The Solid Rock Construction Company

Discovery House
P U B L I S H E R S
BOX 3566 • GRAND RAPIDS, MI 49501

PUBLISHING BOOKS THAT FEED
THE SOUL WITH THE WORD OF GOD.

The Solid Rock Construction Company

How to Build Your Life on the Right Foundation

HADDON W. ROBINSON

The Solid Rock Construction Company
Copyright © 1989 by Haddon W. Robinson
Discovery House Publishers is affiliated with Radio Bible Class,
Grand Rapids, Michigan.
ISBN: 0-929239-08-3

Printed in the United States of America
89 90 91 92 93 / CHG / 10 9 8 7 6 5 4 3 2 1

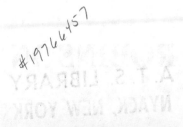

To my precious friend, Bonnie
Who has built a more beautiful house than mine
But on the same foundation.

CONTENTS

THE BLUEPRINT

Addison Mizner, a famous architect and builder of the early twentieth century, designed many houses for the rich of south Florida. Even though he had almost no professional training and one time built a two-story house without a stairway, he had a knack for beautiful homes and was pursued by the moneyed elite. On one occasion a client, William Gray Warden, inquired about getting a copy of the blueprints for his new Palm Beach estate to unveil before friends. Mizner retorted, "Why, the house isn't built yet! Construction first, blueprints afterward."

In many ways Mizner's rejoinder is as much a comment on life as on building philosophy. We are often more interested in the product than the process. Like the Pharisees of the first century, exterior finish is more important than interior. Wandering about from house to house, we check out filigrees but not foundations. Sometimes we need to take a second look. A man's house may be his castle, but not all houses are castles. Some are rotting and crumbling underneath because they were not well designed or constructed. In building lives or houses, we must follow the blueprints; but the architect's drawing is only a guide. No house or life is built without design changes. Yet, if the blueprint is there, we have a goal.

SOLID

My expertise is not in building houses but sermons, yet I know the importance of a plan. After all, good sermons are nothing more than spiritual blueprints. When I was eleven years of age, I went to Calvary Baptist Church in New York and heard Dr. Harry Ironside, pastor of Moody Church in Chicago, speak. After citing the factual details of his sermon in my diary, I wrote this editorial comment: "Some men speak for twenty minutes and it seems like an hour, others speak for an hour and it seems like twenty minutes. What makes the difference?"

I have pursued that question throughout my life, and I suppose that I have listened to or read five thousand sermons in my search. That is one of the reasons I am drawn to Jesus' Sermon on the Mount. That is why I wrote *The Christian Salt & Light Company* and this book, which together study the whole Sermon. What did Jesus say in the Sermon and how did He say it? Those who study preaching, like myself, agree that a good sermon has three basic ingredients.

First, it must have a sense of unity. Things that ordinarily might be separated come together in a oneness that either did not exist or was not recognized before. United States coins have the Latin inscription *e pluribus unum,* "one out of many." A good sermon is a simple truth that comes from many truths. It has unity. This criterion did not come from some back room experts who said, "Let's say that a good sermon has to have unity." It comes from the fact that whenever we see separate things we try to put them together. We go out at night, look up into the sky, and say, "There's the big dipper." What we really see are stars a million light years apart, but our desire for unity brings them together. We see them as a whole. The need for unity is a law of the listener's mind. If a good sermon doesn't have unity, it bothers us. In fact, it ultimately bores us. In houses, sermons, and lives, the pieces fit together.

Second, a sermon has to have order. A sermon is a unit that is preached in time. For us to understand the overall sense of unity, each part of the sermon has to come to us when we need it. It must answer the questions lurking in our minds at just the right time.

Third, a good sermon has a sense of progress, a sense of movement. We have the feeling that the preacher is going somewhere. And we have the comfortable feeling that when he gets there he will stop. He won't keep talking just to fill time.

Unity, order, and progress. I have found all three in the Sermon on the Mount. In fact, one of the reasons I keep reviewing the flow of thought in this book is so readers will see the unity, order, and progress of Jesus' sermon. People who don't see these make ridiculous judgments about its parts. To understand it we have to see it as a whole, in its completeness.

But how do we get unity, order, and progress? To accomplish this a sermon must have a single, central idea. A good sermon is an idea that is expanded and enlarged. Or, looking at it another way, we can compress a sermon into a central thought to give it unity and order. Progress comes as we develop the central thought.

The central subject Jesus developed in the Sermon on the Mount was how can anyone have a righteousness that passes muster with God. What He tells us about that subject is that such righteousness has nothing to do with rules and regulations; it has to do with relationships—a relationship first with God and out of that a relationship with other people. That idea is central to the Sermon. Jesus strikes that note early. "Unless your righteousness surpasses that of the

Pharisees and the teachers of the law, you will certainly not enter the kingdom of heaven" (Matthew 5:20).

The Pharisees were the major league religionists of their day. For them, religion consisted of rules and regulations, responsibilities and duties. But the heart of the problem for many of them was that their religion had no heart. Jesus was saying that if we are going to have a righteousness that meets with God's approval, it has to grow out of a relationship with God and focus on others.

Jesus began in Matthew 5 by giving us the Beatitudes, which are attitudes that characterize people who enter the kingdom of heaven. Those who are beatitude people will be salt and light in a rotten and dark world because their faith will be based on a relationship rather than rules. As they enter deeper into that relationship with God, they will come to understand the truth. To help them understand the truth, Jesus gave six case studies—murder and anger, adultery and lust, divorce and selfishness, oaths and deceit, retaliation and rights, hate and love. In all these cases, Jesus set forth principles that flow from inner righteousness.

In Matthew 6:1 Jesus stated the principle that governs the next eighteen verses. "Be careful not to do your 'acts of righteousness' before men, to be seen by them. If you do, you will have no reward from your Father in heaven." The three acts of righteousness that demonstrate our relationship with the Father focus on giving, praying, and fasting. These acts of worship serve as litmus tests of the reality of our religion. When we perform any of these for show, our religion is a sham.

Giving is something godly people do, but we can give for the wrong reasons. We can give so people will admire us for being generous. If that's our reason for giving, the only reward we get will be a pat on the back.

Fasting is another discipline of godly people. Fasting helps us focus our attention on things that are important. But we can fast for the wrong reasons, too. Some people try to look weak and anemic when they fast so their friends will notice and be impressed with how devout and pious they are. If that's our reason for fasting, the only benefit we'll get from it will be a comment or two from admiring friends.

Righteous people also pray, but they don't have a righteousness that matters with God if they pray loud and lengthy public prayers so others will applaud their spirituality. If we enjoy praying in public so others will admire how marvelously we pray, we have missed the point of the Sermon on the Mount.

Then within this section on prayer, Jesus provides a model prayer. We call it "the Lord's Prayer." Actually, the prayer is misnamed because the Lord Himself could not have prayed this prayer. As the sinless Son of God, He could not join in the petition, "Forgive us our sins." Perhaps the prayer should be labeled "The Disciples' Prayer," since it serves as a primer on prayer for people like us. It helps us in praying as an outline serves a minister when he preaches a sermon, or as a blueprint serves a builder. It guides us as we go.

The skeleton of the prayer opens with an address to God: "Our Father in heaven." The prayer then has two major sections. First, we are to talk to the Father about the Father: His Person, His program, and His purpose—"Hallowed be your name, your kingdom come, your will be done."

Second, having spoken to the Father about the Father, we are to speak to the Father about His Family: the children's need for provision, pardon, and protection—"Give us today our daily bread. Forgive us our debts as we also have forgiven our debtors. And lead us not into temptation, but deliver us from the evil one."

One thing we must do as we work our way through the Scriptures is to understand passages in their context. So the question is, after the Lord's Prayer how does the extended passage of Matthew 6:19–7:12 fit into the context of the Sermon on the Mount? I agree with Robert Guelich that this section stands as a commentary on the Lord's Prayer. Jesus was showing us what a life of prayer looks like.

This extended passage has six sections. The first four begin with prohibitions. For example, in Matthew 6:19 Jesus said, "Do not store up for yourselves treasures on earth." The second section starts at 6:25 with another prohibition: "Do not worry about your life." The third section starts at 7:1: "Do not judge or you too will be judged." The fourth prohibition starts at 7:6: "Do not give dogs what is sacred."

The fifth section beginning in 7:7 is an exhortation to pray based on what has just been said. "Ask and it will be given to you; seek and you will find; knock and the door will be opened to you." And 7:12 summarizes it all with what we call the Golden Rule: "Do to others what you would have them do to you, for this sums up the Law and the Prophets."

Notice how Matthew 6:19–7:12 elaborates on the petitions in the model prayer Jesus gave us. The first section, Matthew 6:19–24 corresponds to the first section of the Lord's Prayer, where we are to pray for God's will to be done, His kingdom to be established, and His name to be honored. In other words, we pray that God will be God to us, that He will be the priority of our lives. The second section, "Do not worry" (v. 25), corresponds to the fourth petition, "Give us today our daily bread." And the third section, "Do not judge" (7:1), corresponds to the fifth petition, "Forgive us our debts as we have forgiven our debtors." And the strange little phrase in Matthew 7:6, "Do not give to dogs what is sacred," corresponds to the last petition, "Lead us not into temptation, but deliver us from the evil one." It is a petition asking God to keep us from Satan's trap, from falling into the hands of the Evil One. The section beginning with Matthew 7:7 exhorts us to pray this way. We are to pray because God, our Father, is a good giver. Then because He gives good gifts, we should also; and this is the basis for the Golden Rule of 7:12.

After Jesus finished His commentary on the Lord's Prayer, he returned to His central theme of how to find true righteousness. He built his case with vivid images—small and wide gates, narrow and broad roads, sheep and wolves, grape vines and thornbushes, fig trees and thistles, good trees and bad trees, rocks and sand. From these images emerge the lonely pilgrim who has taken the road to life, the true prophet who has done the Father's will, and the wise builder who has erected a house upon a rock foundation. These three people reveal in their choices that no true righteousness comes apart from Jesus Christ. He is the Way; through Him we find God. He is the Truth; through Him we know God's will. He is the Life; through Him we have security for eternity.

The illustration of the wise builder is a fitting conclusion to the Sermon on the Mount because lives and houses have much in common. Flesh and blood, as well as brick and mortar, can stand in splendor on an unsure footing. Without the Preacher of the Sermon on the Mount as our solid foundation, we can never live the Christian life, much less understand His Sermon. Life's storms will blow us away. But when we enter into a relationship with Him, when He makes our house His home, we will understand the Master Builder's plan.

ONE

THREE-WAY SERVICE

Henry James and Edith Wharton, novelists published by Scribner's, were good friends, but they were not equally successful in the income from their writings. Because James was quite sensitive about his meager earnings, Wharton often had to plot in secret to help him. She once arranged with Scribner's to offer James an eight-thousand-dollar advance on a new, forthcoming novel with the understanding that the money would be taken from her own book royalties. Because James never learned that Wharton was his benefactor, he received the money with joy.

MATTHEW 6:1–8, 16–18

The Jewish people had a saying for just about everything in life, including giving. One that the rabbis used was "It is better to give nothing than to give to someone and cause them to be ashamed." In other words, if our giving becomes a public display, we risk not only destroying the gift but also hurting the person to whom we are giving it.

The Pharisees, however, did not live up to this cultural ideal of keeping their giving secret. Figuratively speaking, they sounded a trumpet before they gave so that everyone would notice their generosity. Today we would say, "They blew their own horn."

To the Jews, giving ranked as the supreme act of piety. Giving to the needy, said the teachers of the law, was better than sacrifice. When Jesus arrived on the scene He didn't dispute this, but He added a qualifier. More important than giving, said Jesus, was the motive that prompted the giving. He knew the base motives in people's hearts and recognized that even good deeds could be done for bad reasons.

Some people give out of guilt; some give out of a sense of

SOLID

superiority. A friend asks us to contribute to his favorite cause and we feel guilty if we don't. When we help someone, we may picture ourselves as reaching down to help them up. Charity can infuse us with a sense of superiority.

Whether we give out of feelings of guilt, superiority, or for some other reason, most of us want some recognition for our generosity. But if we call attention to our giving, Jesus warned, that attention is all the reward we are going to get.

Jesus said of the trumpet-blowing Pharisees,"They have received their reward in full." This phrase comes from an expression used in ancient Greek commerce. Archaeologists have found it scribbled on papyri identified as receipts and have concluded that it meant "paid in full."

If we give to be seen by others and we receive their applause, we have been paid in full. If we want the praise of men, we can have it; but then God owes us nothing.

If we want recognition from God, however, we should give quietly, not letting our left hand know what our right hand is doing. Then our Father, who sees what we do in secret and knows our motives, will reward us. Good deeds cannot merit more than one payout—if we get our reward from men we will not receive from God.

Jesus was not opposed to having people know about the actions of His followers. Such things cannot always be kept secret or confidential. His concern was that recognition was not His people's motive for giving. He did not want them doing righteous acts for unrighteous reasons.

Fund-raising consultants often approach educational institutions and offer to set up campaigns for these schools. They guarantee that these fund-raising ventures will substantially increase the revenues of the school. Usually their subtle and not-so-subtle strategy includes publishing the names of the people who contribute, listing them in categories according to the amount they donate. Those who give will be trumpeted and by implication perhaps so will those who don't give. These firms raise the needed money and get what they want—a percentage of the take. And the contributors get what they want—their names printed on a plaque or program and the subsequent applause of others. In Jesus' words, they have been paid in full.

If we want public acknowledgement for our righteous acts, we have missed the point of Jesus' message in Matthew 6. This applies to our praying as well as our giving.

When we pray, Jesus warned, don't be like the hypocrites who love to stand in the synagogues or out on the street corners and pray where everyone can see them. Like those who receive accolades for their generosity, these showmen receive their reward in full in being recognized for their piety.

Prayer was as important in the Jewish religion as it is in the Christian faith. When Jews awoke in the morning the first thing they did was pray what was called the Shema: "The Lord our God, He alone is God. Help me to love the Lord my God with all my heart and soul and mind" (see Deuteronomy 6:4–5). At the end of the day, as the sun was setting, they repeated this petition. The Jews also had set times to pray during the day, at 9:00, at 12:00, and at 3:00; and they had specific prayers for different occasions. They prayed a certain prayer when they entered a home, when they saw the sea, and when they viewed a river. They prayed a certain prayer when they entered a city, when they left a city, and when they bought new furniture.

Certainly we can applaud this desire to remember God throughout the day and on each occasion, this zeal to commit every area of life to Him. But there is a danger in much praying, for these frequent prayers can become a kind of automatic reaction or rote response done without thought or meaning. For example, have you ever thanked God for your food before a meal and then been unable to remember what you have prayed, or whether you have prayed at all? This is what happened to many Jews: prayer had become something they went through as a thoughtless routine in their daily lives.

Another thing happened. Perhaps figuring that if they prayed long prayers they could pester God enough to gain His attention, they did just that. Their prayers became longer and longer.

These were the kind of folks who could say, "I spend an hour in prayer every morning." Now there is nothing wrong with spending an hour in prayer if it is time spent in true devotion to God. But God doesn't time our prayers, although some people seem to believe that He does. They operate as if somehow God is sitting in heaven with a stopwatch and He is more impressed with an hour-long prayer than He is with a five-minute prayer.

Whether we are trying to impress God or people, Jesus said, praying for effect is hypocritical. He pointed His listeners to those who repeated a prayer over and over as though it were some magic chant or formula. They were just like the pagans, Jesus said, who babbled their empty litanies, thinking they would be heard because of their many words. When Elijah challenged the prophets of Baal on Mount Carmel (1 Kings 18), the pagan prophets repeated "O Baal, answer us!" for half a day. Centuries later the people of Ephesus did the same thing. Attempting to reach the ears of their goddess, they shouted the phrase "Great is Artemis (Diana) of the Ephesians!" for two hours (Acts 19). For the pagans, prayer served as a magic formula. If they found the correct formula and repeated it often enough, perhaps the gods would respond.

"The fewer the words, the better the prayer," said Martin Luther. And the prayer Jesus gave to us as a model prayer has fifty-seven words in Greek and only fifty-two words in English. Yet this short prayer too is often mumbled thoughtlessly like some rote formula of faith.

Because prayer had a special place in Jewish religion, religious types schemed to get other people to notice their piety. It's easy to see how they worked that out. You're expected to pray at 9:00 and 12:00 and 3:00 and you want to pick up a reputation for being pious. So you make it a point to be in the marketplace at those hours, or on the top step of the synagogue. Then when it's time to pray you assume the prescribed position—arms stretched out and eyes shut—and it is clear to everyone around that you are very devout. Prayer turns into a performance. Several years ago a Boston newspaper reported on a prayer given by a noted clergyman as "one of the most eloquent prayers ever delivered to a Boston audience."

Again, Jesus wasn't opposed to public prayer. He was against the motive that turned it into a performance. That's why He admonished His followers to go to a room and close the door. In the Jewish homes of the first century the only private place where the door could be locked was the storeroom, and that's the word Jesus used. In a private place no one can see us, showmanship disappears, and we are more likely to talk with God.

The motive behind their worship was what mattered. Jesus also applied the principle to the matter of fasting. "When you fast, do not look somber as the hypocrites do," Jesus warned, "for they disfigure their faces to show men they are fasting" (Matthew 6:16). Traditionally, the pious Jew covered his head with ashes when he was fasting. Again, Jesus refuted this traditional practice, warning that those who let their fasting be known in such a manner had played to an earthly audience, and they would only receive the admiration of men and women. If they wanted God's pleasure and reward, they must change their motives and mode of operation.

Interestingly, fasting does not have a big place in the Bible. In the New Testament, it is never commanded; it is only reported. In the Old Testament, the people fasted once each year, on the Day of Atonement (Yom Kippur). We are also told that Moses fasted before ministry, as did Jesus.

So why fast if it is not commanded? In the Old Testament fasting always had to do with acknowledging sin. The people of Israel fasted at times of national repentance. If prayer draws us to God, fasting draws us away from self.

The Homily on Fasting from the Articles of the Anglican Church describes this inward attitude in fasting: "When men feel in themselves the heavy burden of sin . . . they . . . are inwardly touched with sorrowfulness of heart . . . all desire of meat and drink is laid apart."

Many people today seem to look at fasting as a way of winning God's approval. Somehow they think that if God knows how miserable they are without lunch He will be more open to their request. We can't manipulate God. If we fast to wean ourselves away from the ordinary distractions of life so we are more able to concentrate on Him, that's fine—but private.

In the Jewish religion, fasting became theater. The Pharisees fasted twice a week, on Monday and on Thursday. This might have had something to do with the fact that Monday and Thursday were market days when many people came to town. When the Pharisees fasted, everybody in the community knew it. The Pharisees put on a benefit performance for their own benefit. They donned a garment of sackcloth and covered their heads with gray ashes. They wanted the applause of people for their piety, and they got it. They had their reward,

But Jesus told His followers to do otherwise. Wash your face and put oil on your head, He said. Those who really know God should be feasting, not fasting. We ought to wear Easter on our faces, even if we have Good Friday in our hearts.

Giving, praying, and fasting are not things we do for public display. They are private actions done for the good of others or for the strengthening of our own spiritual life. They are private transactions between ourselves and God.

As human beings we want our piety known. It is difficult to give generously and never be commended. It is hard to pray for an hour without letting someone know of our devotion. It is tough to fast—in fact, most of us don't—and not have someone commiserate with our devout hunger. We forget that in all of this there is an important Onlooker who knows all our motives and cares about our true devotedness to Him. He will see that we are rewarded in His own way in His own time.

We get what we go after. If I want good reviews from the critics in my church for the performance of my religion, I can get them. But that's all I get. I get my reward here and now and I am "paid in full." If I want God's approval, I can get that. This Onlooker is not simply a member of the audience or a judge keeping score. He is "my Father in heaven" deeply concerned about my heart's earnest desires. My giving, my praying, my fasting—my worship—is for Him. My Father who knows my deepest wishes will reward me with treasure that I really value.

In *A Christmas Carol*, Charles Dickens described the tight-fisted Ebenezer Scrooge as a man who was "secret . . . and solitary as an oyster." What Dickens expressed negatively about Scrooge, Christ proclaimed to be at the heart of our service for Him. He wanted His followers to carry out their "acts of righteousness" unobtrusively, even secretly at times.

Religion is not a performance; it is faithfulness to a Person. Devotion is not acted out for display and applause; it is our private obedience meant for viewing by our Father in heaven. In our giving, praying, and fasting we are to be in our Majesty's secret service.

TWO

DIRECT CIRCUIT

When my two children, Vicki and Torrey, were young, I played a game with them. I would take a few coins and put them in my hand; I'd show them the coins and then close my hand over them. My younsters would crawl up in my lap and try to pry open my fingers one at a time. Once they captured the coins, they would scream with delight and jump down to treasure their prize. What I enjoyed about that game was having my son and daughter sit in my lap, and feel them close to me. The pennies really didn't mean much to me, but in another way they meant everything to me because during penny play my children laughed and talked with me while I expressed with hugs my deep love for them.

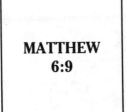

MATTHEW
6:9

When we pray we often concentrate on the gifts in God's hand and ignore the hand of God Himself. We pray fervently for the new job or for the return of health. When we gain the prize, we are delighted. And then we have little more to do with God. If we are only after the coins, God's hand serves only as a way to make the house payment, buy clothes for the children, or pay for the groceries. After the need has been met, the hand itself means little to us.

Although God in His grace does give good gifts to His children, He offers us more than that. He offers us Himself. Those who are satisfied with the trinkets in the Father's hand miss the best reward of prayer—the reward of communicating and communing with the God of the universe.

According to Jesus, when we come to the God of the universe in prayer, we can address Him as Father. Bound up in the word *Father* is a compact summary of the entire Christian faith. It is the answer to the philosopher Lessing's question, "Is the universe friendly?" When Christians bow before God and call Him Father, they are acknowledging that at the heart of the universe is not only ultimate power but ultimate love.

But not everyone can call God Father. It was Jesus who taught us to pray that way. He alone guaranteed that we can enter into a relationship with God and become members of His family.

Some believe in the "Fatherhood of God and the brotherhood of man," but this is not the teaching of the Bible. God is Creator of all, and in that sense we are "God's offspring" (Acts 17:29). But the relationship that a creature has with his Creator is not the relationship of a Father to His children, which is our link with God through Jesus Christ.

In the Old Testament the Israelites did not individually address God as "Father." As far as we know, Abraham, Joseph, Moses, David, or Daniel never fell to their knees in the solitude of their chambers and dared to address God that way. Yet in the New Testament God is called Father at least 275 times, and that is how we are instructed to speak to Him. All that a good father wants to be to his children, Jesus told us, God will be to Christians who approach Him in prayer. We can pray as children. Because of Jesus' death and resurrection, when we come to the sovereign Majesty of the universe, the word that should fall readily from our lips is *Father*.

The address "Our Father in heaven" in Matthew's record of the Lord's Prayer not only recognizes the intimacy that we have with God as our Father, it also speaks of the awe we should have as we come to Him in prayer. The phrase "in heaven" does not refer to God's zip code; it refers to His elevation above all. Jesus was saying that this One to whom we come as Father is the sovereign Majesty of the universe, the God of all power, the God of all authority.

For early Jewish Christians, having a proper awe of God was probably easier than understanding their intimacy with God. Unfortunately, in our day the pendulum has swung to the other extreme. God is often referred to in terms that are anything but awe-inspiring. I cannot conceive of the psalmist saying, "I may not know the answers, but I know the Answer Man." I cannot imagine men and women of the Bible talking about "the big Man upstairs." To say that God is our Father does not imply that God is a great big, huggable teddy bear.

The Bible keeps the tension between intimacy and awe in our thinking about God. The writer of Hebrews said, "Let us then approach the throne of grace with confidence, so that we may receive mercy and find grace to help us in our time of need" (4:16). The fact that we come to a throne should fill us with awe. But because it is a throne of grace, it is approachable. We do not have to parade like the Pharisees or babble like the pagans; we can intimately and confidently talk with our Father.

Yet our Father knows what we need before we ask (Matthew 6:8), so why should we come at all? To put it bluntly, is prayer necessary? Wouldn't it be more pious, more devout, more trusting, to say, "Who am I to tell God how things ought to work?" How will my requests change the course of heaven? Why don't I just leave it up to God and show my trust in Him by not praying at all? Any thoughtful person has asked that kind of question. The answer is in the address itself—"Father in heaven." The sincere cry of "heavenly Father" may in itself be all that prayer needs because we are expressing a relationship of trust and dependence, awe and intimacy. Prayer is not primarily getting things from God but talking with Him.

Being a person is something we hold in common with God, and persons can relate to each other. If a husband and wife are not talking with each other, it is a dead relationship. If a home has become nothing more than a filling station, family life is sterile. Spouses and families need communication and so does every person with God.

We don't come to know God simply because we have feelings. All the beautiful organ music, all the sweet-smelling incense, all the walks down sun-drenched paths cannot substitute for talking with Him and listening to Him as He speaks to us through His Word. When we pray to our Father in heaven, we are communing with a personal God who loves us. The purpose of prayer is primarily to voice to God the priorities of our lives and the needs of our soul. When we talk with Him heart to heart and mind to mind, we affirm our love for each other.

On Father's Day, 1976, my daughter Vicki wrote me a letter. I have saved it and read it several times since then. She wrote in part: "Dear Daddy, Some of the highlights of my life include the days that I receive letters from you. Your letters are always so bright and thoughtful, so loving and so comforting. Since I can't be with you on Father's Day this year, I wanted to write you a note to tell you how much you are valued and loved by me. I enjoy being with you so much . . . You were so fair to me as a child. Unselfishly you seemed to always put my interest above your own. You've always encouraged and expected the best of me . . . I just wanted to tell you that I love you very, very much." No longer did she value me for the pennies in my hand. She had grown up now and treasured better and richer things.

No requests, but communication. Out of communication, communion. That letter expresses a wonderful relationship. Are we blind? Our heavenly Father will do for us more than any earthly father can do for his child. Most of all He wants to bring us into a communion with Himself.

THREE

SKYLIGHT

In the Teutonic language, a forerunner of English, the word *king* simply meant "father, the father of a family, the father of a clan, the father of a people." Eventually, the meaning expanded and implied sovereignty. The original Teutonic meaning of *king* is seen in one of the titles given to kings of England. Charles II, a king who did not have full support of his people, was sometimes announced with the

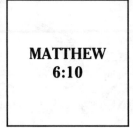

MATTHEW 6:10

epithet "The king, father of his people." But he wanted more than titles. Charles wanted his subjects to truly honor him as a father and gratefully respect his domain and will as a king. He wanted to be set apart in their hearts.

In teaching His disciples to pray, Jesus explained that their view of the heavenly Father's name, kingdom, and will affected their relationship to Him. Jesus told them first to say, "Our Father in heaven, hallowed be your name" (Matthew 6:9). In Hebrew thought, a name was extremely significant. The Jewish people did not give their children names so that their initials would look good on luggage. They didn't choose a name because it reminded them of their Aunt Hilda or their Uncle Harry. Parents chose names for their children hoping that the name would embody the personality, characteristics, or character that they wanted to see developed in the child.

Early American Puritans did that. They gave their daughters names like Silence, Charity, Hope, Love, and Patience. They hoped that their child as she grew to womanhood would live up to her name. We also see the importance of a name in the New Testament. In times of crisis, if a man's life or outlook changed, often his name was changed to match. When Jesus got hold of Peter, his name was Simon.

He was a shifty, sandy, undependable fellow, but Jesus changed his name to Peter, or in effect "Rocky." Jesus renamed Peter before Peter lived up to his new name. It took a while for Jesus to change Peter's shifting personality into rock.

The practice of renaming was seen in more recent days when the cardinal of Poland became the pope. He changed his name to John Paul II because he wanted his life to embody the virtues of his predecessors Pope Paul and Pope John. He chose the name to personify what he wanted to be.

The psalmist proclaimed that those who know God's name will put their trust in Him (Psalm 9:10). He was not claiming that those who can pronounce or read God's name will trust in Him. When we know God's character and His power, we will rest in Him. In hallowing God's name, we are setting it apart, making it something special. We are praying that God may be God to us, that He will be set apart in our prayers in such a way that it will be clear that we reverence God.

Sometimes our prayers are dangerously close to a blasphemy. We often pray as if God were deaf and we have to shout to make Him hear, as if He were ignorant and we have to explain to make Him understand, or as if God were calloused and we have to cajole to get Him to respond. Our prayers betray a very inadequate idea of God.

At other times our prayers reveal that many names on earth are more significant to us than the name of God in heaven. We can be more in awe of an employer, a professor, a loved one, a friend, or a government official than we are of the God in heaven. We can fear a worm of the earth like ourselves more than we reverence and respect the God of heaven to whom we pray.

The petitions in the Lord's prayer cover all that we are to pray about. Whether we pray a short prayer or a long one, we will never pray more than this. Although we often pray for God to increase our devotion and depth of spiritual life, none of these petitions in the prayer is for personal holiness. The first step in spiritual growth is not to pray for inner feeling or inner change but that God will indeed be God in our lives. The focus of the spiritual life is not our inner experience but our honor of God.

We have the command to be holy as He is holy because the spiritual life begins when we determine to allow God to be God in all aspects of life—personal, family, business, recreation—and to allow God to set us apart.

The focus on Him should be true not only in our own inner life but also in our prayers for others. We should not pray merely that others will be delivered from sin but that they will come to know God. The focus of evangelism is not that people will be won to Jesus Christ, as important as that is, but that people in the world who profane the name of God will come to understand who He really is—the God of holiness, grace, and righteousness. And out of that understanding, they will hallow His name.

Wordsworth well expressed the importance of a special relationship with God when he wrote, "Father!—to God himself we cannot give a holier name."

The second request that we direct to the Father about the Father is not devoted to the person of God but to His program. The second petition is "Your kingdom come." Jesus was speaking here about His future messianic reign upon the earth. All through Scripture, the story of the Bible looks forward to the return of the Messiah, Jesus Christ, who will rule in righteousness when the kingdom of this world will become His kingdom.

This concern for God's rule over the earth and its people is basic to our view of history. Joseph Wittig once noted that a person's biography should begin not with his birth but with his death. He argued that we measure the contribution of life not by its beginning, but by its end. That's how we should think about history. Any thoughtful person wonders, Is history going anywhere? Is it a wheel that moves round and round and never touches the ground? Is it simply a cycle of repeated events headed for no destination except perhaps oblivion? Some people shrug off history as a tale told by an idiot, scrawled on the walls of an insane asylum. Edward Gibbon wrote off history as "little more than the register of crimes, follies, and misfortunes of mankind." Ralph Waldo Emerson dismissed history as the "biographies of a few great men." Henry Ford shrugged it off as "bunk."

In the witness of the Bible, however, history is "His story," and history is headed somewhere—the return of Jesus Christ. The Bible anticipates that day when the angels and the redeemed will sing together. Before us shines that light, and the darker the age, the brighter seems the glow.

So when we pray "Your kingdom come," we look toward that glad time when God's messianic kingdom prophesied throughout the Old Testament will be established by Jesus' return to earth. As we pray, we direct our gaze to the day when worldly realms will become His domain.

When we ask for His kingdom to rule, by implication we also pray that the small bit of earth we occupy now will be subject to Him. If we long for the time in the future when Christ's kingdom will be established on earth—enough to pray sincerely for it—then we must be willing for all of the little kingdoms that matter so much to us now to be pulled down. If we want God's rule over all men and women at some future time, it follows that we will want His control in our lives today. Unless we are sufficiently concerned about making our lives His throne and bringing others into glad submission to Him, we cannot pray with integrity for His kingdom to come.

When I was in my twenties, I heard sermons about the second coming of Jesus Christ in which I was exhorted to desire the coming of Christ. Well, I wanted Him to come, but not immediately. I had some things I wanted to do before He came back. I wanted to get married, to enjoy sex, to have children, and to establish a ministry. After I got all that done, it would be all right for Him to return. As I was thinking about this recently, it occurred to me that I no longer have any plans that the coming of Jesus Christ would interrupt. Nothing now takes precedence over His coming. May earth receive her King!

We are to pray for the person of God, that His name will be hallowed; for the program of God, that His kingdom will come; and for the purpose of God, that His will may be done on earth as it is in heaven.

Praying for His will to be done provides a foundation for our prayers. We are basically asking for God's will to be done in our lives and in the world. We often get it upside down, though, and pray as if we expect God to change the way He is running the universe because we have given Him our petitions. We treat Him like a genie in a lamp. When we rub the lamp and make a wish, we expect to be granted what we want.

We must recognize the importance of conforming our will to His will. We shouldn't pray for something and then at the end say, "if it be Your will," if we don't really mean it. These words aren't something to tack onto the end of a prayer as a loophole, as an out, so that if God doesn't give us what we want, we won't be embarrassed. Prayer is not getting God to do my will. Prayer is asking for God's will to be done in my life, my family, my business, and my relationships and in the world as it is done in heaven.

When the Bible gives us glimpses of heaven, we see that the angels stand ready to do God's bidding in heaven; all the hosts of glory respond to His will. In the universe, all the galaxies and all their stars and planets move according to His design. It seems that only here on this third-rate planet, this dirty little tennis ball that we call earth, is there a pocket of rebellion.

For us to live according to God's will on earth as it is done in heaven is to do so in enemy territory. To live in a realm that is controlled by Satan is to recognize that this world is no friend of God's. For us to do God's will on earth as it is in heaven, we must go against the current. When we pray "Your will be done on earth as it is in heaven," we are praying for our friends, our families, our society, but above all for ourselves. We willingly abandon our will to His unconquerable will.

Charles II never completely received the adulation he wanted. His name was associated with too many mistresses and illegitimate children, his kingdom was too frequently divided over various policies, and his will was too often thwarted by a rebellious parliament. He ruled England for over thirty years, but in just three years after his death almost all his achievements were undone.

As Aristotle put it, "They should rule who are able to rule best." That is why we should hallow God's name, long for His coming kingdom, and submit to His will. His rule is best.

FOUR

SUNSPACE

Antonio Sanchez was only five years old when he was sent to a Mexican prison for juveniles after supposedly murdering his baby brother. Tony's parents, who had beaten him with chains and tortured him with fire, deserted him and disappeared after telling police he was the killer. In prison other inmates taunted him with the word *murderer* and sometimes abused him. He had to fight for food. No one seemed to care what happened to Tony, until Carolyn Koons, an American professor, heard his story. She battled bureaucracy and a corrupt prison warden for almost three years before she secured Tony's release and adoption at age twelve, but her real struggles had only begun. Somehow she had to meet the needs of a boy who still stuffed rolls into his pockets because of past hunger, who lashed out at others because of his emotional scars, and who seemed enticed by every wrong because of his unbridled life. As a single parent, she was unsure whether she could meet his physical, emotional, and spiritual needs. But she did because she had a heavenly Father, unlike Tony's earthly one, who understood her needs.

MATTHEW 6:11–13

When Jesus taught us to pray to our heavenly Father, He gave us a model for praying. The first three requests concern God's name and kingdom and will and focus on our Father; then the last three requests about bread, forgiveness, and temptation center on His family.

Helmut Thielicke, a German theologian, pointed out that the whole of life is captured in the rainbow of these requests. "Great things, small things, spiritual things and material things, inward things and outward things—there is nothing that is not included in this prayer."

Adlai Stevenson once remarked, "Understanding human needs is half the job of meeting them." Perhaps the other half is having the will and ability to meet them. God scores on both counts. Because God understands our needs and can truly meet them, Jesus said that we are to talk to the Father about them. After praying about the cosmic and eternal, we can pray about the earthly and temporal.

When Jesus said, "Give us today our daily bread," He was not suggesting a trip to the supermarket for Wonder Bread. He was making the point that it is proper and right to pray for our daily needs. For after all, we cannot really serve His kingdom and do His will unless we have the strength we need for today. So it is proper to ask God for a job to earn money for food. It is appropriate to turn to God for the clothes we need to work on the job to earn money for food. It is also valid to ask for transportation to get us to the job so that we may earn the bread. God knows our needs, and He is concerned about them.

We are often tempted not to bother asking God for food. "Don't pray for groceries," we insist. "Get out and hustle." In fact, some of the church fathers spiritualized the *bread* to refer to the loaf served at communion. They did this, understandably, because after praying for God's glory, it seemed too commonplace to switch to something as mundane as groceries.

Yet, "daily bread" means exactly what it says. The word *bread* refers to the food that sustains our bodies. In the larger sense, of course, bread refers to all that we must have to live. Our Father in heaven concerns Himself with the items on a grocery list. Food for our next meal matters to Him.

The focus of the request is for *daily* bread. The word translated *daily* bewildered scholars for centuries. The Lord's Prayer is the only place that word occurred inside or outside the Bible. Then a few years ago an archeologist dug up a papyrus fragment that contained a housewife's shopping list. Next to several items the woman had scribbled this word for *daily*. It probably meant "enough for the coming day." The phrase should be translated "Give us today bread enough for tomorrow." When prayed in the morning, it is a prayer for the needs in the hours ahead. Prayed in the evening, it is a request for the needs of the coming day. The implication is, of course, that God will supply whatever we need to honor Him and do His will.

In our culture, with its freezers and refrigerators, we seldom purchase food for a single day. We store up food in such abundance that we mutter only thoughtless words of thanks as we eat.

Jesus did not invite us to ask for everything in the Neiman Marcus catalogue, or for a Lincoln convertible, or for Gucci shoes. Pray for bread—the necessities of life, not the luxuries. Ask for bread, not cake. Nor are we invited to request supplies for years to come. We are to ask for the essentials to take us through tomorrow.

Notice, too, that when we pray "Give us today our daily bread," we ask for others as well as ourselves. If I pray this prayer in sincerity, it delivers me from selfishness and hoarding. If the Father supplies me with two loaves and my brother or sister with none, I understand that God has indeed answered our prayers. My extra loaf is not for storing, but for sharing.

God wants to free us. We can bring our small requests to God. We can place before Him our need for bread, a coat, a pair of shoes—all those items that matter to us. If we need them, then they matter to our heavenly Father as well.

After we ask the Father for provision, we should ask Him for pardon. Even though we are instructed to pray "Forgive us our debts as we also have forgiven our debtors," we don't seem to worry much about our sins. Walter Horton speaks to our condition in his book *The Challenge of our Culture*: "Modern man is certainly worried about something—worried nearly to death. And an analysis of his behavior shows him so feverishly trying to avoid looking God in the eye that it must have something to do with the fear of how he must look standing before God in that position." A cartoon in the morning newspaper pictures a psychologist listening to a patient: "Mr. Figby," the psychologist finally says, "I think I can explain your feelings of guilt. You're guilty!"

"Forgive" follows "give," and Jesus linked the two petitions. In that way when we think of our need for food, we will recognize our need for pardon as well. Also, as we confess our guilt, we consider how we have handled our relationships with others.

In Luke 11, the prayer is "to forgive us our sins" (v. 4). The petition in Matthew 6 "to forgive us our debts" (v. 12) recognizes that sin is not only deliberate disobedience but also a debt. It is a debt we owe to God, which Jesus Christ has paid.

Augustine labeled this request for forgiveness "the terrible petition" because if we harbor an unforgiving spirit while we pray to be forgiven in the same way as we forgive others, we are actually asking God not to forgive us.

Think of how the confession of sin works. If I honestly pray for forgiveness, then I revise my estimate of myself downward and I admit my own guilt. If I see the pollution of my own life, then I see the sins of others in a different light. Without that, I can regard myself as so important, so dignified, so honorable that it would be unthinkable to forgive anyone who dared offend someone as righteous as I. That is self-righteousness. To squeeze pardon from a self-righteous prig is harder than squeezing apple juice from a stone slab. It's simply not in such a person to forgive.

If we honestly know God as our Father, then we are part of the forgiven fellowship. Although at times we may find it difficult to forgive someone who has wronged us, we cannot help but see an individual offense as trivial in comparison to our sin against God. When we forgive others, it is evidence that we have entered into God's forgiveness. Men and women who live in the relief of God's pardon find it easier to forgive those who offend them.

We are never more aware of God's grace than when we admit our sin and cry out for pardon. We are never more like God than when, for Christ's sake, we extend forgiveness fully and freely to those who have sinned against us.

Having prayed to God for provision and pardon, we go on to seek His protection and so we pray, "Lead us not into temptation, but deliver us from the evil one."

A young woman in a shopping mall sported a T-shirt that proclaimed: "Lead me not into temptation—I can find it myself." She wanted people to chuckle as she passed, but her one-liner raised a question. What are we praying for when we ask, "Lead us not into temptation"?

Why should we have to ask God not to lead us into temptation? To ask Him to keep us out of temptation would be more understandable. Professor D. A. Carson suggests that Jesus is using a figure of speech to express something positive by stating the opposite concept. For example, if I say, "This is no small matter," I mean it is a big matter. When we pray, "Lead us not into temptation," we are really praying, "Keep me away from temptation." We are crying out, "Don't let Satan ambush us. Don't let the foe of our souls catch us in his trap." We are recognizing that God has the power to lead us past all the lures to sin that threaten us. Therefore, we ask, "If the opportunity to sin presents itself, grant that I will not have the desire. If the desire springs up within me, grant that I will not have the opportunity."

Let's face it. We seldom want to be delivered from temptation. It promises too much fun. Some wag has said, "Don't resist temptation. It may go away and not come back." Temptation stirs the blood and inflames the imagination. If we were revolted by it, it would not be temptation at all. Usually, though, temptation doesn't seem very bad, so we play with it, flirt with it, and invite it into our lives. When we pray about sins, it's not temptation that bothers us. It's the consequences of our disobedience that we want removed.

In the context of this prayer, however, we are not merely asking God to keep us from being naughty boys and girls. The work of Satan threatens more severe danger than that. We are surrounded by ten thousand seductions to live life apart from God. In our ambitions and in our successes we are tempted to honor our own names, to build our own kingdoms, to take credit for baking our own bread, and to deny our need for forgiving grace. The enemy of our souls wants us to cast away from God. Only God can make us see sin for what it is. If temptation brought chains to bind us, we would resist it on our own. Instead, it brings flowers and perfume and offers life and good cheer, good times and enlargement. It bribes us with wealth and popularity and entices us with promises of prosperity and unbounded freedom. Only God can keep us from its charms.

The Lord's Prayer reminds us to fear the strategies of Satan. Years ago Helmut Thielicke said of postwar-occupied Germany, "There is a dark, mysterious, spellbinding figure at work. Behind the temptation stands the tempter, behind the lie stands the liar, behind all the dead and bloodshed stands the 'murderer from the beginning.'"

When we pray "Deliver us from the evil one," we recognize Satan's power, admit our weakness, and plead for the greater power of God.

When we truly sense His provision, pardon, and protection, we will recognize His preeminence over all. The Lord's Prayer, as we commonly recite it, concludes with a trumpet blast of praise: "For yours is the kingdom and the power and the glory forever, amen." Since those words seem like an appropriate and fitting way for the prayer to end, it is somewhat unsettling to discover that the sentence does not appear in the earliest and best manuscripts of either Matthew or Luke. Evidently the doxology was not part of the prayer as Jesus originally gave it. In fact, it appeared for the first time in the second or third century.

Yet the prayer demands a conclusion. Otherwise it stops with the threat of temptation and the warning that the evil one has set his snares for us. When Christians in the young church offered up this prayer to the Father, rather than finish on a cold and frightening note, they added this affirmation of praise.

Although this doxology may not have been given directly by Jesus, it can claim broad biblical support from the words of David (1 Chronicles 29:11) to those of the four living creatures (Revelation 5:13). This paean of praise, however, is not an assumption that we must accept in order to pray, but rather the confidence to which prayer draws us.

Tony Sanchez was not initially drawn to his new mother, Carolyn Koons. In fact, he seemed more drawn to trouble than anything else. He accused her regularly of not loving him and taunted her with "I won't obey you or anyone." Carolyn never stopped barbecuing those juicy hamburgers he craved, never quit hugging him after his acid words, never ceased rescuing him from fights. Carolyn had almost despaired of Tony ever bonding to her; somehow all those daily little things she had done for him seemed to have no impact. But then Carolyn got a big surprise; Tony made an unexpected speech at his junior high graduation. In almost a stutter he said, "I want to thank my mom for adopting me and bringing me to the United States." Then with tears streaming down his face, he yelled, "I love you, Mom. I love you. I love you." All the glory was Carolyn's that day.

When we recognize our Father's daily care for us, experience the depth of His forgiveness, and sense His ever present shield, we shout, "Yours is the kingdom and the power and the glory and I love you, Father."

FIVE

PERMANENT FIXTURES

Jack Perry spent twenty-five years in the U.S. Foreign Service. "We did not enter government service in order to make money primarily," he wrote in *Light from Light*, "but we were usually sad whenever we took stock after another move and found that we were once again in the hole. . . . We never owned the house we lived in because we knew we would be moving again in a short while. . . . After a Foreign Service career, we emerged without riches, but with a strong . . . understanding that physical treasures of this world are not the important things."

MATTHEW 6:19–24

In contrast to Jack Perry, the Pharisees were men of wealth and lovers of money (Luke 16:14). They were not religious professionals, such as priests, but they were religious laymen. Although they made their living in the marketplace, they were known for their strict adherence to the laws of their religious tradition. As a result, they were highly respected and often became wealthy and powerful because of their influence over the people.

Like the Pharisaical viewpoint, the Puritan ethic, the understanding that all work is done before God, has been behind the accumulation of wealth by many in America. In the Puritan ethic if a person plowed a field, he did it as a sacred service to God. If someone molded a sculpture, it was for the eye of God rather than man. People who took their work that seriously, as something they did as service to God, often ended up being very successful. We pursue the Puritan ethic in work today—not to please the Almighty but to get the almighty dollar.

Hard work often pays off, as it did with the Pharisees; but they made a wrong conclusion. They reasoned that their wealth was a reward for their righteousness. In reality, of course, they made a good living because of their good lives, and that is not the same. Early in the Sermon on the Mount, Jesus demonstrated that their righteousness was not true righteousness. It was simply conformity to an outward standard.

So in His sermon Jesus showed them that their riches, which they thought were a reward from God for their piety, were not true riches, and therefore not a true reward. So in many ways the section on storing up treasures connects to the rest of the Sermon on the Mount, but it is primarily an elaboration, or commentary, on the first two verses in the Lord's Prayer. It shows the implications of what it means to pray the first part of this prayer. If we hallow His name and pray for His kingdom to come and His will to be done, that should affect our view of money.

Some devout people have felt that Jesus' warning about not storing up earthly treasures means that we are not to have a bank account or own property. But that is not the witness of the Scriptures. Paul endorses the principle that parents save for their children (2 Corinthians 12:14), and Proverbs lauds the lesson of the ant who stores for the future (Proverbs 6:6). The Bible has a good word for saving.

The Bible also acknowledges the right to own private property. The eighth commandment about not stealing has no meaning unless someone owns something to steal. Peter rebuked Ananias and Sapphira for lying, not for possessing property. He said that their land and the money they received from selling it were always at their disposal (Acts 5:4).

Jesus neither condemned saving nor asked everyone he met to give everything away. He warned about storing up our goods when our motive was to find our security in our possessions. He abhorred the miserly spirit that desired money and stashed it away, forgetting that money is a trust from God. Money is not for keeping score in the game of life. It is to be used to meet needs.

The rich fool of Luke 12 filled his barns with grain, but God judged him for his greed (v. 20). The rich man of Luke 16 could have helped the beggar Lazarus, but he didn't (vv. 19–20). The picture of this same rich man in torment distinctly portrays the foolishness of shortsightedness—investing in ourselves rather than others. Moths, rust, and thieves will destroy our precious possessions anyway.

In the first century banks did not exist, so people saved their wealth in three ways. One was by hoarding garments. A cache of fine garments was as good as money in the bank. They could be sold in the future. Achan stole a Babylonian robe, and God condemned him for it (Joshua 7:20–21). He didn't take an old suit to wear; his apparel snatch was an investment in the future.

A second way of accumulating wealth was to store grain in barns. Famine was an ever present reality in the ancient world of the Near East because of the undependable rains. If a man could store his grain until a famine came and prices soared, he could become fabulously wealthy.

The third method of saving lay in exchanging their assets for gold. Instead of locking it in a bank vault, however, they hid it in a pot or buried it in a field.

Jesus pointed to the ways rich people held their possessions and warned that there were no safe investments. For a gourmet moth beautiful garments make a splendid menu, and garments with holes become a lost investment. Grain could be eaten. The word *rust* is just the word *eating*. It is sometimes used for rust because rust eats away at metal, but in this passage it might more naturally refer to the eating done by such rodents as rats and mice. Thieves can steal gold by breaking in, or more literally "digging in." In fact, the thieves in the first century were called diggers. The Palestinian houses were made of baked clay, so a burglar broke in by digging a hole in a wall. People may think their garments, grain, and gold appear secure, but moths, mice, and marauders can demonstrate that earth has no secure investments.

Two thousand years have passed. The situation may have changed but the reality hasn't. Stocks and bonds are at the mercy of a changing market. Inflation, like a rat, can nibble away at a bank account. Currency can be devalued. Houses, boats, and cars are subject to fire, tornadoes, and rust. Even land can lose its value with just one chemical spill. Wherever we put our wealth, there are no guarantees. Only short-sighted investors build up portfolios on this earth. Jesus gave better advice on investments. Equities built up in heaven are more secure and bring better dividends. In the context of the Sermon on the Mount, those who give to the needy are supporting God's work in the world. What we invest in people remains because people are eternal.

Origen, the church father, described Christians as money changers, taking the capital of earth and changing it for the currency of heaven. In other words, we need to invest our wealth in that which will outlast us. The Koran puts it another way: "When a man dies, people on earth ask what did he leave? The angels in heaven ask, what did he send ahead?"

We are to put our treasure in heaven not only because that which is eternal will last and that which is temporal will fade, but also because it will give us the right focus. Notice Jesus is not saying that our treasures follow our hearts. It's the other way around. Where we put our treasures our hearts will be. How can we cultivate a heart for God? By putting our investments in the right place. It's a fact of life that our interests follow our investments.

Investors who play the stock market check the quotes daily to see how their stocks are doing. Although they seldom analyze every stock on the exchange, they rarely miss their own. That is where their concern lies. It goes without saying that with every investment there is a corresponding interest.

If we want a zeal for His eternal kingdom, we must put our treasure there. If our lives are consumed with building a business, buying a nicer home, or trading for a new car every year, God and His kingdom get little more than a tip of the hat or tip money. What is more, if we center our lives on the junkbonds of earth, we find dying difficult.

Samuel Johnson, the eighteenth-century English lexicographer, was once invited to tour a mansion, a place of magnificent beauty surrounded by manicured lawns. As Johnson was leaving he remarked to a friend, "A place like this makes it difficult for a man to die." The more we store up here, the more calamitous death appears. Because we leave behind what we have valued most highly. Put it down as a principle of life—wherever you have your treasure you will have your heart.

People who live for the here and now, who can total up their treasures by their bank statements or their real estate investments, live for this age because it is the only age they know. This is all there is. But those who know the reality of God's kingdom understand that Jesus was not making a fund appeal or cozying up to a big giver; He was talking sense.

When we gain an eternal viewpoint, our earthly perspective is never the same. After all, our viewpoint is all important.

A man in New York City had a wife who had a cat. Actually, the cat had her. She loved the cat. She stroked it, combed its fur, fed it, and pampered it. The man detested the cat. He was allergic to cat hair; he hated the smell of the litter box; he couldn't stand the scratching on the furniture; and he couldn't get a good night's sleep because the cat kept jumping on the bed. When his wife was out of town for the weekend, he put the cat in a bag with some rocks, dumped it in the Hudson river, and uttered a joyful good-bye to the cat. When his wife returned and could not find her cat, she was overwhelmed with grief.

Her husband said, "Look, honey, I know how much that cat meant to you. I'm going to put an ad in the paper and give a reward of five hundred dollars to anyone who finds the cat."

No cat showed up, so a few days later he said, "Honey, you mean more to me than anything on earth. If that cat is precious to you, it is precious to me. I'll tell you what I'll do. I'll buy another ad and raise the ante. We'll increase the reward to one thousand dollars."

A friend saw the ad and exclaimed, "You must be nuts; there isn't a cat on earth that is worth a thousand dollars."

The man replied, "Well, when you know what I know, you can afford to be generous."

If we have any inkling of what it means to be part of God's kingdom, we can afford to be generous. We can establish priorities by the way we give and live.

The importance of having an eternal perspective is what Jesus illustrated with his eye examination. "The eye," He said, "is the lamp of the body. If your eyes are good, your whole body will be full of light. But if your eyes are bad, your whole body will be full of darkness. If then the light within you is darkness, how great is that darkness!"

At first glance that illustration can confuse us. Behind it stands a kind of childlike simplicity. Our eyes resemble lamps that illuminate the inside of us. When we close our eyes, everything inside goes dark. When we open our eyes, light floods in and everything inside seems lighted. If we have good eyesight, the light shines in and it is bright inside of us. But if we have bad eyes, it is as though everything inside us becomes gray and dim. And if we lose our sight, everything inside us is midnight.

Jesus used the eye to symbolize our perspective on life. Putting it another way, if our perspective is eternal, we walk in light. We are not likely to stumble because we see things as they really are. We recognize the difference between the eternal and the temporal. But if we don't see well, if our perspective is temporal, we're likely to trip over every little obstacle, every minor temptation.

Jesus concluded that people whose minds are fastened on the temporal usually think they are in the light. And that, He said, is tragic.

In a sense, they are like people who have been blind from birth. They learn to get around and to "see" in their own way. They become independent and sometimes resent sighted people who tell them which way to go, try to help them, or warn them about obstacles. They have their own reality, their own way of perceiving the world.

We live in a world where people not only spend their lives on what is temporal and give themselves to that which does not last, but they defend it as reality, as light. Men and women believe that this life is all there is and promote their philosophy. Jesus lamented that if we confuse darkness with light, our darkness is very deep.

Our perspective is either one of light or of darkness. And if we can't tell the difference, it's disastrous.

Our perspective, either light or darkness, determines our priorities, which in turn motivate our service and our giving. Jesus warned that we cannot serve two masters, both light and darkness, God and money.

Some people, when they hear this, think Jesus was warning us about moonlighting. Since thousands of people work two jobs, one during the day and another in the evening, they conclude that Jesus was exaggerating when He said it is impossible to serve two masters. It may be difficult, but certainly not impossible.

But Jesus wasn't commenting on working for two employers. He was describing the problem of being a full-time chattel slave to two masters. A first-century slave was the property of the master. He belonged to the master all day and every day. He didn't work for eight hours and have the rest of his time to himself. He did whatever his master wanted him to do, whenever he wanted it done.

If a man got into the impossible situation of becoming a slave to two masters, he would soon learn that he cannot respond to both of their demands. Either he will hate the one and love the other, or he will be devoted to one and despise the other. In near eastern thought the concepts of hate and love have little to do with emotions and feelings. They focus on devotion and priorities. In other words, if a man ends up being a full-time slave to two masters, he will have to turn his back on one of them. The demands of the job make it impossible for him to honor both.

The slave must decide which master he will serve. That choice resembles in the sense that when we love one person, we say no to all others. When a man marries a wife, it doesn't necessarily mean that he harbors emotional animosity toward the girls he didn't marry. It's just that the job of marriage requires a twenty-four hour commitment.

Chapter Five

You can't dance to the music of two orchestras at the same time. You can't be married to two people simultaneously. You can't worship in the temple of two separate gods. And you cannot serve God and money.

In many translations the word *money* is *mammom*. The NIV uses money because nobody knows what mammon is. It was an Aramaic word that had to do with possessions, with property. It is not necessarily a negative word. Money becomes negative when it gets out of place, when we end up serving it instead of using it.

We all serve something. Something governs our lives, determines our priorities, dictates how we spend our time, affects our daydreams, writes our definition of success. The only question is, What will we serve?

You can serve money in reality and God in pretense. You can serve God and use money, but you can't serve them both. That's a statement of fact. So the question is, Do you serve God and use money, or do you serve money and use God?

If we pray "Our Father in heaven, hallowed be your name, your kingdom come, your will be done on earth as it is in heaven," a major application of that prayer has to do with our pocketbooks. When we invest our money in what is eternal, that has a way of affecting our hearts. If we work and walk in the light we see things for what they really are and we realize that the things that are seen are temporal and the things that are not seen are eternal. And when we hold that priority, we will serve God.

How can we know if we are mastered by our money? A couple of questions come to my mind. First, how did we get the money? Did we sacrifice something eternal to get it? If so, we have become a slave to money. Would we put a competitor down and destroy him to be sure we got what was due us? If so, money is determining our priorities. Second, what do we do with our money? Let's put it bluntly. Is the cause of God in the world better off because we have been entrusted with money? Or does God only get our spare change?

A boy on his way to church had two quarters—one for the offering and the other for a candy bar. While crossing the street he tripped and fell, and one of his quarters went rolling out of his hand and into the sewer, ker-plunk. Later he told his father what had happened. "Did you put the other quarter in the offering?" his father asked. "No," the boy said, "God's quarter went down the sewer."

If we suffer a financial reversal and we change our budget accordingly, does God and God's work get eliminated? What stands at the top of our budget? Where does God fit in our priorities?

This passage about treasures, eyes, and masters was Christ's commentary on the first three petitions of the Lord's Prayer. When we pray, "Hallowed be Your name," we are saying, "Let God be God to me," and we promise to invest everything we possibly can to see "His kingdom come, His will be done on earth as it is in heaven."

Praying the Lord's Prayer has implications that go deeper than mere words; they reach right into our pocketbooks.

In the game of Monopoly, players buy land and collect money. When one player has enough money and at least one monopoly of properties, he or she can buy houses and hotels and collect rent on them. Eventually one player receives enough rental money through land and building holdings to bankrupt the other players, thus ending the game. Parker Brothers, the makers of Monopoly, take for granted one final instruction—when the game is over, put all the pieces back in the box.

Chapter Five

People who live for the present, who spend their strength on what cannot last, are like children who play Monopoly as though it were reality. In the end, we all get put in the box and we are gone. What matters is what remains when the game on earth is over.

SIX

PRESSURE TREATED

Death was walking into a city one morning when a man stopped him and asked what he was doing. "I'm going into the city to claim ten thousand people," Death answered. "That's horrible," said the man. "It's terrible that you would take ten thousand people." "Look," Death said, "get off my back. Taking people when their time has come is my job. Today I have to get my ten thousand." Later, as Death was coming out of the city, the man met him. Again he was furious. "You told me this morning that you were going to take ten thousand people, but seventy thousand died today." "Don't get on my case," Death said. "I only took ten thousand. Worry and anxiety killed all the rest."

MATTHEW 6:25–34

It's true that worry can make us sick. It may even be possible to worry ourselves to death. When we worry, we don't worry with our minds, we worry with our organs. And if we worry long enough and hard enough, we will get ulcers and make ourselves vulnerable to all kinds of other sicknesses. Worry can sometimes even cause us to commit suicide. Gallup ran an interesting study a couple of years ago with young people in the United States. When teens were asked what their major feeling about life was, sixty percent replied, "Fear." That may explain why suicide among teenagers has become a national epidemic. In the last decade, suicide among teenagers has gone up almost four hundred percent. People worry about AIDS; we ought to worry about suicide. It ranks as the second leading cause of death after accidents for young people under twenty.

People do all kinds of things to handle their worries. *Time* magazine a couple of years ago said that Americans gulp

SOLID

down seven tons of sleeping pills every day. We gulp down sedatives and tranquilizers until the drugs turn us into addicts.

Other people turn to alcohol. A good stiff drink or a couple of cocktails make their worries seem smaller and make them feel bigger. Edward FitzGerald, in *Rubáiyát of Omar Khayyám*, described that prescription for worry when he wrote, "Ah, my Beloved, fill the Cup that clears Today of past Regrets and future Fears." But when I see the commercials for alcohol rehabilitation centers, it becomes clear that taking a good stiff drink to handle our worries may really give us something to worry about.

People in Jesus' day had just as much anxiety as we do. Some may think life was easier in the first century because the times were simpler and people didn't have as much to worry about. But anyone who thinks that doesn't understand conditions in the first century. Most of the people in the ancient world lived like members of the third world today. Laborers were paid every day because they needed the money to live the next day. The government gave them no security. They had no safety net. Some estimate that the average citizen in Palestine paid at least forty percent of his wages in taxes. Times may be hard today, but they were concrete tough then. Yet to people then and now, Jesus said, "Don't worry."

Jesus began His discussion of worry with the word *therefore*, so we know it is related to what Jesus spoke about previously. If we take seriously the Lord's Prayer, He said we will be concerned about where we put our treasures. If we are concerned about God's kingdom and that which is eternal, we will not be had by what we have.

What we value determines how we live. If we have double vision—if we look intently on earth and try also to look at heaven—we will stumble and fall flat on our faces. We have to choose. If we value that which is eternal, we will choose to serve God. If we value that which is temporal, we will serve money. The fact that we will serve something is taken for granted; we give our lives to something. What that will be is up to us.

If we commit ourselves to Him, He commits Himself to us. If we become a slave to God, He will free us from anxiety and worry. This also ties into the fourth petition of the Lord's Prayer. Having prayed that God's will and His kingdom will be first in our lives, we can then pray, "Give us today our daily bread." That privilege alone should remove worry from our lives.

God committed Himself to two things. He committed Himself to what goes into our bodies: food and drink. And He committed Himself to what goes onto our bodies: clothes.

When Jesus declared "Don't worry," He didn't mean we shouldn't think about tomorrow. The *King James Version* translates this as "give no thought for tomorrow." The verb really means "don't give anxious thought." That is, don't worry about it. Jesus was not against thinking about tomorrow. That is part of being human. We are not warned against forethought but against foreboding.

"Don't worry" doesn't mean "Don't work." Jesus used birds as an example. Every self-respecting bird works hard for food and shelter. But it doesn't worry. In fact, when Paul wrote his second letter to the Thessalonians, he said, "If a man will not work, he shall not eat" (3:10). God is not against working; He is against worrying. He was saying to His disciples, "Don't worry about the necessities of life." If we commit ourselves to Him, He commits Himself to us.

That sounds good on paper, but Jesus' words may give us the uneasy feeling of someone patting us on the back and saying "Don't worry" just after we have totaled our only car. Words by themselves don't calm anxiety. But Jesus didn't stop with the command. He followed it with seven reasons in support of a worry-free life.

Jesus took His first reason for not worrying from the logic of creation. Life is more important than food and clothing. If God did the greater thing—gave us life and created our bodies—surely He will do the lesser thing—give us food to sustain us and clothes to keep us warm. If God has done the big thing, we can expect Him to do the little thing. For instance, if a jeweler gave you an expensive diamond ring as a gift, would you not expect him to give you a box to put it in?

"Is not life more important than food, and the body more important than clothes?" Jesus asked. We may not appreciate the full force of this argument because we are not sure it is true. We tend to get our self-identity from what we eat and what we wear. We are no more than birds or lilies. Advertisers reinforce this belief. The underlying message in many advertisements is that we are what we wear or eat.

But Jesus said we are more than that. God gave us life, and He will surely give us what we need to stay alive.

Worrying about the basic necessities of life is not only needless, Jesus concluded, but secondly it is also senseless. At our house we have a bird feeder. Sometimes I watch the birds while I eat my breakfast. Few people work harder than birds. I never see robins sitting on a branch hoping that heaven will drop a worm into their mouths. I see them scratching and pecking to find their meals. But they don't worry. They sing. Jesus wasn't suggesting that we not work. He was saying, "Be like the birds who don't worry." Their Creator takes care of them and your heavenly Father will take care of you.

Nor was He proposing that we stop sowing, reaping, and storing away in barns. God is not against farmers or farming. He was simply reminding us how much better off we are than the birds. They can't sow, reap, or store, yet they don't worry. Why then, He asked rhetorically, should we who have these abilities spoil our lives with worry?

Behind this argument about God's provision for the birds stands the Bible's model of the universe. In this model God stands outside the universe and also within the universe. This view says that God created all things and sustains all things. He designed the universe to act according to certain laws of nature. We who are in this universe can observe what is happening and learn those laws. In fact, that is our commission. We are the keepers of the universe. We are the ones to whom God has given the mission of guarding what He has made.

This view is not mechanistic—it is not tied strictly to scientific laws or cause and effect relationships—for God, if He chooses to do so, can break into that universe and set aside the natural laws. He did so when He raised Jesus from the dead. God created the universe, sustains it, and can overrule it when necessary. It is held together by His sovereignty, by His power.

There are two distortions of the biblical model of the universe. One is deism, which views God as the creator of the world but not necessarily as the sustainer. Deists believe that God made the universe in the same sense that a watchmaker makes a watch. When He finished, He went off to make other watches and left the universe to tick away on its own. When we discover the laws that keep the watch ticking, we learn about an infinite God; but this view leaves no room for a personal God.

The second distortion is seeing God as sustainer of the universe but not recognizing Him as creator. These people are much like the pagan animists, the people who believe that what they do affects the gods or spirits and that the gods or spirits in turn affect the people's lives. Animists believe the gods are capricious; they can be happy one day and sad the next. But by pacifying the gods, they can get the gods to bless them.

Like these animists, many well-meaning Christians believe God's work in their lives is always immediate. For them, everything is a miracle, even finding a parking place on a crowded city street. They have three miracles before breakfast, five before lunch, and another six in the afternoon.

Instead of having spirits to placate, these Christians placate God. The laws of nature do not mean a great deal to them. They see God as sustainer, but they don't acknowledge His work as creator because they don't recognize that God works according to the laws of nature He established at creation.

The implications of a proper view of the universe are amazing, almost overwhelming. In the biblical view God is infinite—He is above His creation—but He is also personal—He is involved in His creation. This understanding of the universe recognizes science as well as miracle. It says that the universe runs according to laws. In addition to the natural laws that govern the universe, there are moral laws that govern human behavior. In a moral universe we can discover things about the way people live and the results of their behavior. When we acknowledge that behind the universe stands a righteous God who has set His physical and moral laws in motion, we acknowledge that we don't break God's laws. We simply break ourselves on His law.

When Christians look at nature, they see evidences of God's providence and design. In this example Jesus implied that God provides for the birds of the air as part of His process of creation. That is His way of sustaining birds, and He sustains us in much the same way. He gives us the brains, the bodies, and the forces of nature necessary to provide for ourselves. That is why we thank Him for our food. When pagans hear us thank God for our meals, they may think we believe that He brings food directly to our tables. But when we thank God for food, we do not thank mother nature but our heavenly Father who provides for us through the processes set in motion at creation.

If God as creator and sustainer has set in order the process to feed the birds, surely He has made provision to feed us as well.

The third reason Jesus gave for not worrying is that it is useless. Worrying won't add a moment to our lives nor an inch to our height. In other words, it doesn't change anything. Worry does nothing to meet our basic needs. And since it is useless, we ought not worry.

People who have read *MAD* magazine recognize Alfred E. Newman as the fellow with the good-natured smile whose motto is "What, me worry?" He is not so confident or secure that he has no reason to worry; he is simply a dolt who does not have enough sense to worry.

A friend of mine has a plaque in his office that says, "If you can keep your head when all around are losing theirs, it is obvious that you don't understand the situation."

It is true that some people don't worry simply because they are mindless. Certainly Jesus was not commending people who are thoughtless, reckless, shiftless, and who neither work nor think. Too much of the Sermon on the Mount applauds people who take life seriously.

But some folks take life far too seriously. In fact, they are so careful about life that they let it fill them with care and anxiety. These folks can blow a small incident into major proportions. They turn worry into a life-style.

People like that sometimes come to me for counsel. If I show them how to solve a problem they argue with me. "Yes, but . . ." they say, and then they bring up something else. I get the unsettling feeling that they don't want to stop worrying. These folks always live with worse-case scenarios. If they read about a problem with Social Security, they are certain they will not only lose their benefits but will have to pay additional taxes as well. They worry about the bank failing, and if it doesn't fail they worry whether or not they have enough money in it. They worry about their investments, their family, their friends, and the nation's summit conferences.

The way we look at life, Jesus said, has a lot to do with how much we worry. If we focus our attention on temporal things, such as bank accounts, careers, and physical appearance, we have reasons to worry. For example, if we build an extensive wardrobe we'd better worry about moths. They can make a great dinner out of woolen suits. If we have a big bank account, we'd better worry. The bank could fail tomorrow. If we find security in our house, we'd better worry. The house might catch on fire. If we stockpile treasures to put inside our houses, we'd better worry. Professional thieves can break into any house. Everyone who focuses on earthly things has reason to worry.

On the other hand, if we focus on that which is eternal— God's kingdom and His work in the world—our hearts will be at ease. As we commit ourselves to God, He commits Himself to us. And He promises that if our hearts are where His heart is, He will take care of our needs.

The fourth reason we should not worry is because it is

faithless. "Why do you worry about clothes? See how the lilies of the field grow. They do not labor or spin. Yet I tell you that not even Solomon in all His splendor was dressed like one of these. If that is how God clothes the grass of the field, which is here today and tomorrow is thrown into the fire, will he not much more clothe you, O you of little faith?" (Matthew 6:28–30).

The flowers Jesus spoke about were ordinary field flowers, red poppies or anemones that still grow in Palestine. They are like wild grass. As a fuel for baking bread a housewife would gather this grass, cut it, let it dry, put it in the oven, and then light it. It would make a hot fire for an instant or two, just long enough to heat the oven. She would then remove the burned grass and put her loaves into the heated oven until they were baked. Although the grass was good for nothing but making a fire, God dressed it in great beauty— more splendid than one of Solomon's robes. Solomon dressed himself, but God dressed the flowers.

Jesus not only compared grass to Solomon's finest attire but also to people. Grass is passing, but people are permanent. We will live some place forever. And if we belong to God, we are not only permanent, we are of special value to Him. So the contrast is great. If God clothes the passing flowers in great glory, surely He will give us who are permanent an ordinary wardrobe.

When Jesus said we have little faith, I think He meant that worry shows our faith to be insufficient and thoughtless. Some people have sufficient faith to believe God will get them to heaven but not enough to believe He will get them through the next twenty-four hours. They are absolutely confident of the sweet by-and-by but are terrified by the nasty now-and-now. Others thoughtlessly focus on everyday events but forget the ultimate issues of life.

The fifth reason we should not worry is because it is god-less. Worry shows that we are little more than pagans. The Jews considered the Gentiles pagans because they believed in lesser gods or in no god at all. The mythical gods of the Greeks and Romans were insufficient gods that lied, cheated, got angry, murdered, and were actually less than human. To the Jews, those gods were the opposite of the God of righteousness.

Worrying was natural for the Gentiles because they couldn't trust their gods. Our worry testifies that God cannot be trusted, that the God we worship is no different from the gods of pagans. This is a form of atheism and an affront to God.

The absence of worry ought to distinguish people who live for what is eternal. We are people who trust in God, and that should make a difference in the way we handle life.

The sixth reason we should not worry is because worrying denies family ties. Jesus made plain that our heavenly Father knows our needs. The emphasis throughout the Sermon on the Mount is that the God we trust relates to us as our heavenly Father. We belong to God and to His family. Therefore we ought not worry because God will do no less for us than a good earthly father would do for his children.

The Jews of the Old Testament did not think about God this way. No one in the Old Testament called God *Father*. They did not pray to Him as a heavenly Father. But again and again Jesus told us that our Father is God, that God is our Father. When He introduced the Lord's Prayer in Matthew 6:8, He said, "your *Father* knows what you need before you ask him." He followed that by saying we are to pray to our *Father* in heaven. When He spoke about the way we should give, pray, and fast, He said that our *Father* who sees in secret will reward us openly. Then He told us that our heavenly *Father* feeds even the birds of the air.

The fatherhood of God is a constant emphasis in the Sermon on the Mount. This is incredibly significant. It means that at the heart of the universe is not only ultimate power but also ultimate love. We are part of God's family. We bear the family name. And God has committed Himself to us as a father commits himself to his children. As children we don't always know what we need. Sometimes we confuse necessities and luxuries, but God gives us what we need. Sometimes we ask for things that could destroy us, but our Father doesn't give us those. God does for us what a good earthly father does for his children. If we believe this is true, we have no reason to worry.

Because we are our Father's children, if we worry about anything it should be about His kingdom. Jesus pointed this out with a touch of humor when He said, "Do not worry about tomorrow, for tomorrow will worry about itself" (Matthew 6:34). He had been talking about misdirected concerns that grow into worry. In this statement He took a slightly different approach. He acknowledged the human propensity to worry and said we should at least worry about something important. If we're going to have concern, we should have it about big things, about things that concern God, like God's kingdom.

Again, this ties into the Lord's Prayer. The first section of the Lord's Prayer deals with praying to the Father about the Father—that His name will be hallowed, that His kingdom will come, and that His will will be done. Then we can ask for daily bread. In other words, we are to seek His kingdom first, to make that the aim of our lives, and then these things will be given to us, leaving us no reason to worry.

The word *seek* was used to describe the activity of a hunter who hides in a blind to hunt birds. He is hunting for food, not just for sport. He focuses his mind on those birds. His eye always looks for them. He keeps his bow and arrows ready. The birds will be within shooting range for only a moment, so he is constantly alert.

Just as a bird hunter makes birds the center of his attention, we are to make God's kingdom the center of ours. Then all we need, in addition to His kingdom and His righteousness, will be given to us. And that too takes us back to the context.

Righteousness is what Jesus has been talking about. He said, "Unless your righteousness surpasses that of the Pharisees and the teachers of the law, you will certainly not enter the kingdom of heaven" (5:20). Then He explained that the righteousness we are to seek has nothing to do with keeping rules and rituals; it has to do with relationships. It has to do with our relationship to God, which is kept in tact with pure motives, not outward motions, and with right attitudes, not religious acts. This righteousness is shown in the way we perform religious deeds—giving, praying, and fasting. We don't do them for applause; we do them for God and for His kingdom. To seek His kingdom is to seek His work in the world. To seek His righteousness is to live the kind of life that pleases Him, which leads to another truth about righteousness. It has to do with our relationship to others. A righteous life seeks the highest good for others. Whether we deal with foes or friends, we seek their highest good because that is what God does. In business affairs or family affairs we are to seek the best for others. As we seek what is best for others, God gives us what is best for ourselves.

And so we must choose. Will we continue to worry about our own needs or will we decide instead to fasten on God and His kingdom and trust Him to give us what we need? To choose earth is to lose everything; to choose heaven is to gain everything. If we live only for earthly things, we lose heavenly things; if we live for heavenly things, we get earth thrown in.

Worry is needless, senseless, useless, faithless, godless, pointless, and last, it is impractical. "Each day has enough trouble of its own" (v. 34). One of the most difficult things to do is to live one day at a time. People keep ruining all their todays by mixing spoiled yesterdays or unripe tomorrows into their stew. Some people live with yesterday's slights, grudges, and guilt. Something bad happened to them, and they can't forget it. Other people live with tomorrow's threats, evil, and sorrow. Something fearful might happen to them, and they can't ignore it. Helmut Thielicke called this "wandering in times not our own."

If we don't live a day at a time, Jesus argued, we spoil all of life. God divided life into bite-size chunks called days, and trying to chew more than one at a time can choke us.

People seldom, if ever, are destroyed by what happens on one particular day. What really does us in is our worry about what might happen tomorrow.

A farmer drawing water from his well started to wonder what might happen if his well went dry. Before long his wondering turned to worrying. Soon he couldn't enjoy the water he had because of his concern that he might not have any the next day.

God can't control that kind of worry; He can't help us with the future until we get there. And when we get there it is no longer tomorrow; it is today. And God has promised to take care of our todays. He told us to pray for bread daily, not weekly or monthly. If He can supply our needs for one day, He can do it for every day and every week.

And the reality is, most of the crises we anticipate never happen at all.

Wally Morgan, a friend of mine in Dallas, is fond of repeating, "Don't tell me worry doesn't do any good. When I really worry about something it doesn't happen! "

Ian McLaren asked, "What does your anxiety do? It doesn't empty tomorrow of its sorrows, but it empties today of its strength. It does not allow you to escape the evil, but it renders you unfit to cope with it when it comes."

Jesus was telling us not to let tomorrow's worry affect today. Doing so only robs power from today. Can we trust God to supply our needs for the next twelve hours? The next twenty-four hours? That is all He has committed Himself to. Every time we bite off a hunk of today, God commits Himself to meet our needs. And when we think of it, that is all we need; no crisis has ever happened in the future.

On the way to his inauguration, Abraham Lincoln stopped in New York City, where he spoke with Horace Greeley. Greeley asked Lincoln the question that was on everyone's mind. "Will the nation be plunged into a civil war?" Lincoln responded to Greeley's question with an anecdote about some lawyers from Illinois. They followed the judge from town to town to argue cases. As they traveled they had to cross a number of rivers, including many that were swollen. They were particularly worried about the Fox River. In a small town where they had stopped for the night, they met a circuit riding preacher. He had crossed the Fox River many times, so they asked him about it. "I have one rule that helps me cross the Fox River," he said. "I don't cross the Fox River until I get there."

SEVEN

TOLERANCE

"You can't be a Christian," the female caller said to Dr. Gordon Lewis, a professor at Denver Seminary. "Jesus said, 'Judge not that ye be not judged,'" she continued. "And here you are judging whether or not a cult or some individuals are really Christians." Dr. Lewis, who specializes in the study of cults, was on a Denver talk show to discuss the New Age movement. During the program listeners were invited to call and ask questions. Many of the callers asked about particular cults and wanted to know whether or not they were Christian. In a warm and gracious way, Dr. Lewis had been answering their questions.

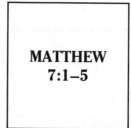

**MATTHEW
7:1–5**

The woman's accusation put Dr. Lewis in a difficult situation. He could not defend himself without getting into a lengthy discussion of Matthew 7, and a talk show wasn't the place to do it. Apparently the woman was unaware that later in Matthew 7, Jesus warned His listeners to beware of false prophets. "Watch out for false prophets," He said. "They come to you in sheep's clothing, but inwardly they are ferocious wolves" (v. 15). I don't know any way to beware of false prophets without making some judgment about prophets and their messages.

A few years ago, a friend who is a pastor in Southern California heard that a treasurer in his congregation was having an affair. He asked the man if it were true. The man admitted it and added that he felt it was a very positive addition to his life and he had no intention of repenting. Later the pastor and an elder of the church, a respected and godly man, confronted the treasurer again. They pointed out his sin and the damage it was doing. The man still refused to change his ways. They took the matter to the leadership of the congregation, and they asked the man to appear before them, which he did. But in an arrogant and defiant way, he said that for the first time in his life he had found out what true love was and he was not about to give it up. And so, reluctantly, the church excommunicated him. The man did not take it easily. He went through the community saying that the pastor and congregation were unchristian because they were judging him. They had no right to do it, he claimed, because Jesus Himself said, "Judge not that ye be not judged."

I suppose no sentence in the Bible is more familiar, more misunderstood, and more misapplied than "Judge not that ye be not judged."

Leo Tolstoy, who was intent on applying the Sermon on the Mount to society, decided that Matthew 7:1 was a basis for getting rid of law courts. According to his interpretation, judges and juries act in direct disobedience to Jesus when they judge who is wrong in a legal matter.

Part of the problem here is deciding what we mean by judging. In both Greek and English the word has a multitude of meanings. Sometimes it means a simple evaluation. And sometimes it means censorship and condemnation.

Is Jesus saying it's wrong to judge a cake-baking contest? A talent competition? Is it unchristian to give a recommendation for a student who wants to go to college? Is it sinful to evaluate someone who applies for a job? Are employers wrong to give their employees job reviews?

The only way to answer these questions is to determine what Jesus means by *judge*. And the only place to find His meaning lies in the context of what He said. To understand the context we need to review what Jesus has been preaching in His mountainside sermon.

It begins in Matthew 5 with the Beatitudes—the attitudes that ought to characterize men and women who are part of

Christ's kingdom. Jesus says that beatitude people, in contrast to the Pharisees, who were very good at keeping rules and regulations, are concerned about inner righteousness.

The righteousness that characterizes people who belong to Jesus has nothing to do with externals; it is an inner relationship with God that shows up in relationships with people. It changes the heart first, not behavior.

For example, in 5:21 Jesus said that if we are really concerned about being righteous we don't draw the line at murder, we draw it at anger. We recognize anger as the internal counterpart to murder, and as followers of Christ we deal with it.

The same is true of adultery. In verse 27, He said we should not be content simply because we have never committed the act of adultery. Lust is the internal counterpart to adultery. If we take Jesus seriously, we will be as concerned about lust as we are about adultery.

Oaths were another example of the conflict between motives and actions. People in the first century had oaths that mattered and oaths that didn't matter. They were like children who promise something and then say it doesn't count because they had their fingers crossed. Jesus said we're not to do anything like that. When we write contracts we're not to focus on every word and punctuation mark to allow ourselves loopholes to get out of keeping our word either in letter or in spirit. Our biggest concern should be honesty and integrity. When we say yes, we mean yes. When we say no, we mean no.

In Matthew 5:38, Jesus talked about revenge. We are not to try to get back at people. We're to deal in generosity. We don't say, "We invited them over last time. It's their turn to invite us." Or "I picked up the check last time. This time it's her turn." Instead we are generous. If someone asks a favor, we do more than she asks.

Finally Jesus said we are to be people of love. No matter whom we deal with, we are to seek that person's highest good. We love other people.

The point of all this is that we are to have inner righteousness. Christ has called us to a righteousness of motive, not a righteousness of rules and regulations.

In chapter 6 Jesus turned His attention from principles of righteousness in relationship to the law and dealt with the practice of righteousness in relationship to religion. He singled out three acts of religious people. They give, they pray, and they fast.

We're not to do them so that others will notice and think well of us. If we do, that's all the reward we will get. If we want a reward from God, we will do these things in quietness so that only He will know.

Beginning in 6:19 Jesus elaborated on the Lord's Prayer. He began a series of negatives: "Do not store up for yourselves treasure on earth" (v. 19); "Do not worry about your life" (v. 28); and now "Do not judge or you will be judged" (7:1).

Matthew 7:1 is an elaboration of the fifth petition in the Lord's Prayer: "Forgive us our debts, as we also have forgiven our debtors." And the commentary in 6:14 says that if we forgive others when they sin against us, our heavenly Father will also forgive us. But if we do not forgive others their sins, our Father will not forgive ours.

What Jesus meant by judging therefore is the opposite of forgiving. To judge means to condemn people rather than forgive them. When Jesus said, do not judge, or you too will be judged, He was saying that as His followers we must not have a spirit of condemnation toward other people. Or a spirit of harsh criticism. A spirit that puts other people down. That kind of judgment often characterizes people in our society and it comes out of self-righteousness.

The reason we criticize people, the reason it is great sport to point out other people's faults, is that by pulling others down we think we can build ourselves up. If we point out someone else's sickness, we think we highlight our health. If we point out another's failures, we think we showcase our successes. Harsh and vitriolic criticism that condemns and judges is the mark of a self-righteous person trying to gain a righteous reputation by delighting in the faults and flaws of other people. But once we recognize our own poverty of life and our own sinfulness, once we recognize our own desperate need and have come to hunger and thirst for the righteousness of God and have cast ourselves with reckless abandon upon His grace, we will no longer condemn or judge.

So when Jesus said, "Do not judge, or you too will be judged," He meant that a person who manifests a critical, judgmental, condemning spirit is a person who doesn't know God at all. He still stands under God's judgment. A forgiven person is a forgiving person.

Two things are important here. First, we are to look at the manner of our judgment, at the measure we use. In the same way we judge others, we will be judged. When we make judgments about other people, what is our attitude? Is it one of forgiveness or condemnation? Is it an attitude that shows concern for the person and a desire to restore him? Or is it an attitude that wants to use her fall as a step to raise ourselves?

If we judge with an attitude of putting people down, God will put us down. If we judge with an attitude of helping other people, God will help us. What measure we use will be measured to us.

The rabbis would say that God deals with two measures: the measure of mercy and the measure of justice. That was a common saying in the first century, and I think that is what Jesus meant. We can judge in mercy or in justice. If we want justice for others, we'll get justice for ourselves. If we want mercy for other people, we gain mercy for ourselves.

When we judge we usually say that what we want is justice. But when we judge someone, when we deny them our forgiveness, we put ourselves in the place of God. We intimate that we don't have that weakness, that failure; we imply that we occupy a position of perfection. And none of us dare make that kind of judgment on another person. All of our judgments are partial at best. We don't know the entire story of anyone else's life.

When a man fails to resist temptation and falls into sin, we don't know, can't know, how much temptation he resisted before he fell. In fact, if we understood the whole story instead of criticizing him, I think we'd often commend him for his courage. All of our judgments are not only partial, they are fallible. Even when we know the facts, we are not always right in our verdicts. That's why we have hung juries. Twelve honest and true people look at the same facts presented by the same attorneys, and some see guilt while others hold out for innocence. Hung juries loom as constant reminders that human verdicts are fallible.

We have no basis for judging or demanding justice. Yet we do it. And if this attitude dominates our lives, we are on dangerous ground.

If a man commits adultery we know he has sinned. The Bible prohibits sexual looseness. But what is our manner? What is our measure of judgment? Is it one of condemnation? Do we insist that the sinner be punished? If so, do we apply that standard to ourselves? Perhaps we haven't committed the act, but again we may not have had the opportunity. Maybe we have kept our uniform clean simply because we haven't had a chance to get into the game. What about our fantasies, our reading, our thoughts? What about the things we'd do if we had the chance? If we demand justice for others, we expect strict justice for ourselves. Or do we?

If we have a co-worker who is a liar, how are we to respond? We can't simply say lying doesn't matter; it does matter. But do we respond in mercy or justice? If we are concerned about her lying, are we equally concerned about our own? Do we shade our stories to make ourselves look good? Do we change the facts a bit to bolster our case? Do we cheat on our income tax or change our expense accounts? If we insist on justice for our co-worker, then we must expect justice for ourselves.

Our attitude toward other people and their sins speaks volumes about our attitude toward ourselves and our standing before God. A forgiven person is a forgiving person.

Frankly, when I stand before God I don't want justice, I want mercy. But only those who give it will receive it. Mercy is a family trait.

After showing us the absurdity of being judgmental, Jesus showed us what hypocrites we are. "Why do you look at the speck of sawdust in your brother's eye and pay no attention to the plank in your own eye? How can you say to your brother, 'Let me take the speck out of your eye,' when all the time there is a plank in your own eye?" Jesus pictured a person with a tiny speck of sawdust in his eye, which of course can hurt and irritate. Then along came an ophthalmologist to remove the speck, but a huge log sticks out of his eye. It was an absurd scenario. It sounds like a comedy routine. But in life itself it comes close to reality.

When the prophet Nathan told king David a veiled but pointed story about a sheep thief, David flew into a rage. The king had a keen conscience about stealing sheep, but somehow he didn't have any conscience about stealing wives. He was trying to remove a speck of sawdust from a man's eye when he had a log in his own. It happens all the time.

A businessman convicted of embezzling hundreds of thousands of dollars from his corporation resembled a mother bear guarding her cubs when it came to the petty cash box. Every day everyone had to account for every cent they took. While he monitored the trickle of petty cash, he was pulling the plug on the corporate bank account. He was big on other people's accountability but oblivious to his own.

Not long ago a preacher in Maine had an affair with a woman in his church. The story made national news because he had campaigned against pornography. He had preached against it and led campaigns to abolish it in his community. He was death on sexual loosness in magazines but apparently blind to it in his own life. The man railed against the sawdust of the Seven-Eleven down the street but could not see the telephone post sticking out of his face.

Jesus did not contend that sin in other people's lives was unimportant. He simply pointed out the absurdity of concerning ourselves with a speck in others without paying attention to our own plank.

So what are we to do? Jesus said, "You hypocrite, first take the plank out of your own eye, and then you will see clearly to remove the speck from your brother's eye" (7:5).

The word hypocrite is close to our word for actor. Jesus called this kind of judgment hypocrisy because it pretends to show a concern for righteousness. Hypocrites feel righteous when they spotlight the sins of others. To them, the essence of religion is concern about sin, but someone else's sin, not their own. If we are really concerned about sin, and we ought to be, we will first of all be concerned about our own. If we are really concerned about righteousness, we will be concerned about righteousness in ourselves. To be concerned about another person's sin and not our own is to playact religion. We play a part designed to impress an audience, but we don't care much about authenticity in our own experience.

After we remove the plank from our own eye, we have two things going for us. First, we can see clearly the sin in someone else's life. Second, we are in a position to help that person deal with that sin.

If we take seriously the sin dogging our own lives and come to the poverty of spirit such insight gives us before God, that affects the way we look at sin and how we deal with it.

When we let God operate on the sin in our lives, that changes the way we deal with people. When we see their sin in the light of what we have wrestled with, we approach them in a spirit of grace and concern. We can encourage others to repent because we know the agony of sin and the relief of God's forgiveness. Oswald Sanders captured what Jesus meant: "What God has done for me, he can easily do for you. You have only some sawdust in your eye, but I had a huge log in mine."

That spirit of grace is what Paul spoke of when he said, "If someone is caught in a sin, you who are spiritual should restore him gently" (Galatians 6:1). The *King James Version* says we are to "restore such an one in the spirit of meekness." Where does meekness come from? It comes from sensing our own desperate need for mercy and from knowing the work of God in our own lives. Knowing how God has handled us, we can minister gently to others. We approach them not as a judge to condemn, but as a brother or sister to restore.

A good place to look for a post in your own eye is to take a look at whether you judge others. Do you frequently pass judgment? Why do you do it? How do you do it? If you do it out of a sense of condemnation, you have put yourself in the place of God. And that's about as far from God as you can get. You cannot know the mercy of God and refuse to extend it to others.

Colonel Protheroe, the magistrate in Agatha Christie's *Murder at the Vicarage*, didn't have much patience with law-breakers. In fact, he thought they should all be punished alike, without exceptions.

"Firmness," he said to the vicar. "That's what is needed nowadays—firmness! Make an example. If you catch someone on the wrong side of the law, let the law punish him. You agree with me, I'm sure."

"You forget," said the vicar, "my calling obliges me to respect one quality above all others—the quality of mercy. When my time comes, I should be sorry if the only plea I had to offer was that of justice. Because it might mean that only justice would be meted out to me."

EIGHT

WRECKING CREW

In the 1700s missionaries from the London Missionary Society faced a multitude of obstacles and temptations in the South Pacific. Many of their problems on the island of Tonga came from other Europeans, who considered the missionaries a threat to their freewheeling life-style. One of their tactics to under-mine the work of the missionaries was to taunt them and mock them for their sexual purity. George Veeson, one of the ten missionaries on Tonga, could not with-stand the pressure. He gave in and joined the Europeans in their promiscuous life among the natives. He took land, servants, and a harem of wives.

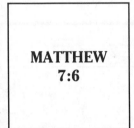

MATTHEW 7:6

But he did more than that. He disgraced himself, the London Missionary Society, and God.

Through the centuries, many committed Christians have turned their backs on God when their passion for short-term personal pleasure has blinded them to the long-term cost.

Jesus warned us about giving in to these inevitable temptations when He said, "Do not give dogs what is sacred; do not throw your pearls to pigs" (Matthew 7:6). In other words, we are not to throw our lives to the world and invite humiliation and scorn.

Many commentators have wrestled with this verse and been thrown to the mat by it. They are not quite sure what it means. Jesus had been talking about not judging. And a little later He talked about asking, seeking, and knocking. But sandwiched in between sits a warning about dogs and pigs. What did He mean?

The metaphor itself isn't hard to understand. Dogs and pigs were despised animals. The dogs we read about in the Bible were not like the cuddly creatures that jump in our laps to have their heads scratched. They were scavengers, more like wild animals than pets.

When Jesus cryptically pronounced, "Don't give what is sacred to dogs," He was referring to the meat offered to God in the temple of Jerusalem. The temples we know of today are much different from those in the first century. To get the right idea about temples we must clear our minds of images of St. John the Divine in New York or St. Peter's in Rome. The temple in Jerusalem may have been a beautiful structure, but at its center was a slaughterhouse. The Jewish people who came to worship brought animals and sacrificed them to God to show Him they were serious about their sin.

At the end of the day not all the sacrificial meat had been consumed, so something had to be done with it. But no one was quite sure what. If they put it in the garbage heap, scavenger dogs would spend the night ripping it apart and eating it.

We have somewhat the same problem today with old flags that are worn and tattered. How are we to dispose of them? Out of curiosity I called the Air Force base and asked one of the officers what to do with an old flag.

"Well," he said, "in an appropriate ceremony, you could burn it. Or you may wrap it and bury it. One thing you don't do—you don't throw it in the dumpster because other people will throw garbage on it and you will desecrate the flag."

I have the same problem with worn-out Bibles. I have a collection that I don't know what to do with. They are too torn and tattered to give away, but I don't feel right throwing them in the garbage. I don't want to desecrate them because the book means so much to me.

The priests had that problem. So they took great care to burn the meat and bury it so scavengers would not get it.

Those who have lived on farms know that when you feed pigs they squeal, push, and shove to be first at the food trough; they pay no attention to Miss Manners or Emily Post. If for some insane reason you would feed them pearls instead of grain, the pigs would go after it thinking it was something to eat. But as soon as the swine realized the pearls were not grain, they might go after you.

Like dogs and temples, first century pigs were different from the plump, well-scrubbed Miss Piggys we think of today. They were half-wild creatures derived from the European wild boar, and they didn't sing love songs to Kermit the Frog.

Knowing this, it's not hard to figure out that Jesus was warning us not to give something sacred and valuable to those who won't recognize or value it. But what is not so easy to figure out is what all that had to do with everything else Jesus was saying? Why did Jesus say that at that particular place in his sermon? And when He was talking about dogs and swine, whom did He have in mind?

We get some help from the Bible in the references to dogs and pigs. For example, speaking about the death of Christ a thousand years before the crucifixion, the psalmist wrote, "Dogs have surrounded me; a band of evil men has encircled me" (Psalm 22:16). David, a righteous man who was being persecuted, foresees our Lord on the cross surrounded by those who, with great delight, pinned him there. And they are like a pack of savage dogs, circling, ready to jump, ready to tear the victim apart.

And in Philippians 3:2, Paul wrote, "Watch out for those dogs, those men who do evil, those mutilators of the flesh." Even more interesting is the discussion of false teachers in 2 Peter 2. Peter compared them to dogs who return to their vomit and to washed sows who go back to wallowing in mud.

Unless we somehow change the inner nature of a dog or pig, the dog will revert to form and delight in vomit and the pig will thrive on mud baths.

Apparently the dogs and pigs Jesus called attention to in this part of His sermon were people in opposition to Him and His message.

So we're back to our question: How does this sentence about dogs and pigs fit the context of what precedes and follows it?

Some commentators say the verse refers to evangelism, that we ought to be discriminating as to whom we tell the Good News about Jesus Christ. We ought to be sure we're not giving it to people who will scoff, mock, jeer, and despise it.

There are times when it is wise not to speak, when it is better to let your life say something before your words, to let people hear the music before you sing the lyrics. This is especially true when people are mocking. I was on a plane awhile ago and a fellow next to me and a fellow across the aisle had had too much to drink. One of them saw me studying my Bible and asked if I believed it.

"Yea, I guess I do," I answered.

"Don't touch him," said the guy across the aisle. "If you start attacking him you'll tear him apart, and that poor guy is going to lose everything that he holds dear."

"Do you want to get into a discussion," I asked. "Do you want to argue? Tell me the kind of life you are living. You're drunk. You can't even hold your own beer, and you're telling me you are better off than I am. By all means, let's talk about it."

I wasn't evangelizing. In that conversation it would have been ridiculous for me to give them the gospel. I wanted to say, "Look, if you think you have something better than I have, I'll listen to you." It wasn't the right time to throw the gospel before those two men. There had to be something done before that.

There are times, even in evangelism, when it is wiser to be quiet than to speak. And sometimes in the silence there is a great deal of eloquence.

This is a fairly common view, and there is some support for it. Luke 23 tells how Jesus stood before Herod prior to the crucifixion. Herod was eager to interview Jesus. He wanted to ask Him many questions, and he hoped Jesus would perform a miracle. But Jesus answered him not a word. Herod was not an ignorant person. He already had more than he was living up to. He simply had a heart of stone, so Jesus refused to answer him.

So there is some support for this view from the ministry of Jesus. Jesus didn't tell everything He knew to everyone He met. Bishop Gore used to say, "Don't shriek the highest truth of our religion on the street corners." There is wisdom in that. A lot of common sense. To present God's truth to mockers who blaspheme and degrade it can be like offering pearls to pigs.

But is this what Jesus is saying here? Jesus has been warning about judging, and He goes on to talk about prayer. Why would He stick in two sentences to urge us to be careful about whom we evangelize? What does witnessing to the Gentiles have to do with the Sermon on the Mount?

Early Christians referred this passage to the Lord's Table. When they gathered for Communion an elder would begin it by saying, "Holy things are for holy people." This food, this bread, this wine, were not offered to anyone who happened to drop into the service.

The *Didascalia Apostolorum*, the oldest book of church order we have, gave this instruction: "Let no one eat or drink of the eucharist, that is the communion service, except those baptized into the name of the Lord. For as regards to this the Lord has said, give not that which is holy to dogs!"

It wasn't that early Christians did not desire to win men and women to God. They simply wanted to keep the fellowship pure. Engulfed by paganism, they labored to keep what was distinct about their faith separate from the influences that would have swept in, immersed it, and destroyed it.

The principle of not giving what is sacred to dogs could apply to the communion, but the question remains: Was that what Jesus meant here? Was He talking about the Lord's Table? If He was, the lesson appears at a strange place. No where else in the Sermon on the Mount did He mention the Eucharist. Although it is not an impossible application, it doesn't appear to fit the context of this passage.

There is another direction we can take to interpret this verse. It grows out of the broader context of the Sermon on the Mount. These two verse go back to the beginning of chapter 6, where Jesus gave us a model prayer.

The final petition in the Lord's Prayer is "lead us not into temptation, but deliver us from the evil one." It was a prayer for protection from Satan, who isn't particularly concerned about whether we commit adultery, murder, lie, or steal. His mission focuses on anything that separates us from the Father.

Satan appears as an angel of light Paul tells us. He fell because he wanted to be like God. Satan's finished product is often a church deacon or elder who lives a very righteous life but doesn't have much trust in God. Self-righeousness serves his purposes as well as unrighteousness. And as long as the Evil One can lure us from God, he doesn't care how well behaved we are.

Jesus once said to Peter, "Satan has asked to sift you as wheat. But I have prayed for you" (Luke 22:31) That's what Satan wanted to do. In the last petition of the Lord's Prayer, we are to pray for protection from the Evil One. As commentary on this request Jesus warned, "Do not give dogs what is sacred; do not throw your pearls to pigs" (Matthew 7:6). He was concerned that we not turn our backs on the Lord and give what is sacred—our lives—to dogs, that we not take what is precious—our relationship with God—and throw it to pigs who will tear us apart.

Jesus made essentially the same point in Matthew 5, where after speaking about persecution He declared, "You are the salt of the earth. But if the salt loses its saltiness, how can it be made salty again? It is no longer good for anything, except to be thrown out and trampled by men" (v. 13).

When I was a chaplain with the Dallas Cowboys, one of the team members came to faith in Jesus Christ. Even though professional football is a tough arena to serve Christ in, this man demonstrated a changed life. Several months later the team was in Philadelphia playing the Eagles and a couple of the guys on the team struck a deal with a call girl. They gave her one hundred dollars and said, "If you can get that guy to go to bed with you this weekend, we will double it, and you can have anything he gives you."

I am happy to report that my friend withstood the tremendous temptation. When he told me about it he said, "I didn't know what was coming off, but they were watching me. They would have ripped me apart if I had gone to bed with that girl."

He was right. They would have ripped him apart. Because they wanted to believe that what happened in his life wasn't worth having. That it wasn't real. But it was. Life is not cheap; it is sacred.

If we turn our backs on our commitment to Christ and dishonor Him, the world outside will be like a pack of ravenous dogs, like a pack of boars that will tear us apart. They will trample us and what we believe into the dirt.

If a man who has followed Christ decides to turn his back on Him, we might think that those people who don't know God would say, "Welcome home, friend. We're delighted to have you back." But they don't. They tear him apart.

When I was teaching at another school, I had a student who was very gifted. He went through seminary and became a pastor of two churches that both grew during his ministry. But then he committed a very serious crime. He was caught and convicted. I have kept in contact with him in a penitentiary in Texas. When he went before the judge, the judge said, "You are supposed to be a Christian. You are despicable. I have only contempt for somebody like you." In a recent letter he wrote, "I am despised by the other prisoners who are here. They go out of their way to cut me down because of who I was and what I have done. I am here for ten years; I don't know if I can take it."

His experience simply confirmed what Jesus said. The convicts in that penitentiary have comitted crimes worse than his. Some of them are in for life. Some serve sentences for murder. But they take great delight in attacking him, like dogs devouring meat or pigs turning on someone who feeds them pearls.

The most difficult thing to handle when talking to scoffers who have no time for God is that they throw up all the Christians they know or have read about whose lives betray the Savior. Like dogs and pigs, they take great delight in savaging Christians.

People living a trivial existence justify themselves by despising righteousness. As a result they revel in followers of

Christ who have fallen into one of Satan's traps. A Christian's sin makes them feel superior. They can behave like pack of wlld dogs or ravenous swine. When a Christian falls for a seduction of the Evil One, they rejoice.

Some non-Christians know this phenomena so well they draw back from following Christ because they are afraid they can't hold out. They hesitate to take on a commitment they couldn't carry out. The truth is, no one can hold out. That's the purpose of the Lord's Prayer. We fight in a spiritual battle and evil men will attack those being attacked by the Evil One. We can't go it alone.

How do we protect ourselves? By a constant dependence on the Father in heaven. He will protect us from the Enemy who schemes to separate us from Him. That explains why we must fervently pray this final petition in the Lord's Prayer and why Jesus goes on to urge us to keep on asking, keep on seeking, and keep on knocking. The price of victory is constant vigilance.

Martin Luther understood what Jesus was saying and captured it in the battle hymn of the Reformation.

A mighty fortress is our God,
A Bulwark never failing;
Our helper He, amid the flood
Of mortal ills prevailing.
For still our ancient foe
Doth seek to work us woe;
His craft and power are great,
And armed with cruel hate,
On earth is not his equal.

Did we in our own strength confide,
Our striving would be losing;
Were not the right Man our side,

The Man of God's own choosing.
Dost ask who that may be?
Christ Jesus, it is He;
Lord Sabaoth is His name,
From age to age the same,
And He must win the battle.

NINE

DOOR KNOCKER

"Irving Berlin has no place in American music. He *is* American music," said Jerome Kern. America's favorite songwriter did not earn that distinction by composing a tune every now and then. Berlin has written as many as fifteen hundred songs. "Berlin's songs are his life," said *Time* magazine on the occasion of Berlin's one hundredth birthday. One of Berlin's nine rules for composing a song is "work and

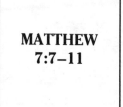

MATTHEW
7:7–11

work and then WORK." Irving Berlin knows all about persistence in songwriting. Jesus urges us to have this same persistence when we pray. In Matthew 7:7–12, Jesus motivates us to pray. He urges us to persevere. Ask, seek, and knock are three different ways of talking about prayer. In the Old Testament, asking and seeking have to do with finding the mind of God Jeremiah 29:12–13 uses those two words together. Although earnest may include repetition, Jesus' emphasis is on persistence, not vain recitations.

What is not captured well in English is that each of the words—ask, seek, and knock—are in the present tense, which denotes a continued action. It is more like a motion picture than a snapshot. The verbs here mean we are to keep on asking and it will be given to us. Keep on seeking and we will find. Keep on knocking and the door will be opened. The emphasis is not merely prayer but persistence in prayer. Pray about different things, but be persistent.

In any discipline, spiritual or physical, repetition enables us to perfect it. Florence Joyner did not become an Olympic runner by jogging around the block once a week. Ansel Adams did not become America's leading black-and-white landscape photographer by taking a few snapshots of his family. Magic Johnson did not become the NBA's most valuable player by shooting baskets only when the weather was nice. It is the nature of any discipline, physical or spiritual, that we persist at it to do it well. We practice again and again. And so Jesus was coaching us to persist in prayer.

We are not to keep at prayer because God needs to be nagged into a response. It is the opposite. We are to persist, to keep at it, because God has committed himself to answering our requests.

The bride-to-be was late to the wedding rehearsal. The groomsmen were getting a bit impatient so they began to kid the groom. They told him she wasn't coming. "Let's all go home," they said. "You might as well call the whole thing off."

But the groom waited. The couple had made a commitment to one another, and he knew she would arrive. He persisted because of his confidence she was coming.

The emphasis here is that we are to persist because God has promised to answer. "Everyone who asks receives," He said. The word *everyone* is limited by the context. This is not a blanket promise. When He introduced this section on prayer in chapter six, Jesus pointed to the hypocrites who prayed three times a day in the marketplace. They pray to be seen, but Jesus made it clear that God made no promise to them. The He described the pagans who babble the same phrase over and over again. They look for the magic word to move their god's heart. They persist, they stay at it, of course, but that kind of useless repetition has no effect on the true God. *Everyone* here refers to the disciples to whom He was speaking, those who wanted to make God's rule paramount in their lives.

A century or so ago people sometimes closed their letters with the phrase "Your obedient servant." That close strikes us as odd, old fashioned, and even insincere. After all, the letters were not written by servants, and we suspect the writer had no intention of obeying the person to whom he wrote. But then our "Yours truly" isn't much better. I get a letter from the IRS signed "Yours truly." I don't believe that. I may belong to them, but they don't belong to me. And it's not enough to be *yours*, we must be *truly* yours. That's about as meaningful as getting a valentine from boys at the garage.

But in a sense prayer resembles a letter to God, a letter of petition. And those who close that letter with "Your obedient servant" are His disciples. The people who say to God, "I am truly yours, I want to be your person." That is the kind of person to whom this prayer is addressed. To those who persist in prayer because they believe God answers and who want what God wants for them.

So the first thing Jesus indicated was that we persist because we believe God has committed Himself to answer us. That means prayer is dangerous business. In fact, if we took that promise alone, we would be afraid to pray. Sometimes on my knees I ask for ridiculous things. Sometimes I catch myself asking God for what could destroy me. So Jesus said, "Which of you, if his son asks for bread, will give him a stone? Or if he asks for fish, will give him a snake. If you, then, though you are evil, know how to give good gifts to your children, how much more will your Father in heaven give good gifts to those who ask him!"

The imagery is clear. And the pictures are interesting. The stones He mentioned are found in Palestine, on the shores of the Dead Sea or the Sea of Galilee, and in the wilderness. They are all over Israel. They are small, white stones that have the shape and color of small loaves of bread. But would a father give his hungry child a stone instead of bread? Or a snake instead of fish? No.

Jesus meant that we don't have to be afraid that God will give us something harmful, something that will destroy us. God won't mock us like that. This was a new thought to the Greeks. They believed their gods often mocked them. In fact, in one Greek legend, Aurora, the goddess of the morning, fell in love with a handsome mortal named Tithonus. Zeus asked Aurora what she wanted for a wedding present. She asked that Tithonus might live forever. Zeus granted the request. But Aurora had not thought to ask for her husband to stay young forever. So Tithonus got older and more feeble, but he couldn't die. Because Aurora asked foolishly, Zeus mocked her.

Jesus assured us that God doesn't do that. We have a heavenly Father who is willing to answer and wise enough to give us what we need. The emphasis is on God's wisdom. We often don't know what to ask for. But God knows what we need.

When our daughter Vicki was a baby, she had a habit of waking up in the middle of the night. When she woke up she didn't want to be alone, so she made enough noise to wake up the household. I'd go staggering into her bedroom.

"What do you want, Vicki?" I would ask.

"I want my bear."

I would go find something that looked like a bear and give it to her. She would take one look at it and throw it on the floor.

So I would try again. "Vicki, just tell daddy what you want."

"I want my dolly."

So daddy would go looking for a dolly, return to her bedside, and place it gently beside her. She would hold it for a minute and then throw it on the floor with the bear.

By this time my wife Bonnie had gotten up and gone into the kitchen and warmed a bottle. As soon as she put it in

Vicki's mouth, Vicki was silent. That was what she wanted all along. She had been hungry but was too young to know what would satisfy her. I am convinced that Vicki thought she wanted a bear and thought she needed her dolly. But what she really needed was a mother who knew that she needed warm milk.

When we lay our requests before God, we can ask Him for things we think we really want and be assured that God will not give us something that will hurt us. He will answer according to our needs, as any good father would. Even though we are imperfect, we want to give our children good gifts. But our heavenly Father does even more. We don't always know what to give our youngsters, but our heavenly Father knows exactly what we need.

A while ago I sat with a good friend whose son had kicked the traces. He had been convicted of trafficking in narcotics and was about to go to the penitentiary for a ten-year sentence. I sat with that father, a man of wealth and influence, in his living room.

"You know, I've given him everything he ever asked for," he said. "I think that is what destroyed him."

That father loved his son. I have no doubt about it. And what the boy asked for he received.

"I can't hold this back from my son," I had heard him say. "He knows I have the money to give him whatever he wants."

And so the boy was given his heart's desires, but he was destroyed by the gifts. Fathers don't mean to do that. But they sometimes do.

God does not indulge our whims, but He will give us what we need. As the sage put it:

I asked for strength that I might achieve; he made me weak that I might obey. I asked for health that I might do

SOLID

great things; he gave me grace that I might do better things. I asked for riches that I might be happy; he did not give them so that I might be wise. I asked for power that I might have the praise of men; I was given weakness that I might feel a need of God. I asked for all things that I might enjoy life; I was given life, that I might enjoy all things. I received very few of the things that I asked for; but I received the things that I had hoped for.

In the act of prayer we acknowledge that we can't go it alone. When we ask, a Father answers. When we seek, we find a Father's face. When we knock, a Father, not a servant, opens the door. It's the Father, and we need to know that. Prayer is our way of knowing that.

What do all children need? They need a father's love and care. We look at a boy from a wealthy suburb and say he has everything, everything except his dad. The father has given his son a catalog of expensive gifts, but hasn't taken the time to give him himself.

What do we really need? Gifts? Yes. God knows we need bread and fish to eat. But what we really need is God. If we persist in music, sports, or business, we may gain recognition and wealth; but the greatest gift from persistent prayer is God Himself.

TEN

LEVELING ROD

"I love to have enemies. I fight my enemies. I like beating my enemies to the ground," said Donald Trump, whose name has become synonymous with glitz and greed. His get-even game plan stands in glaring contrast to what we know as the Golden Rule, a commonly accepted moral standard that some have called the Mount Everest of ethics. "Do to others what you would have them do to you" (7:12) is, I am sure, the most famous statement that Jesus made. Folks who know very little about the Bible know the Golden Rule. But it isn't original with Jesus. The rule, in one form or another, goes

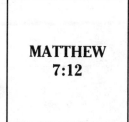

MATTHEW
7:12

back centuries before Christ. Isocrates, a Greek philosopher who lived about five hundred years before Jesus, used it. Socrates gave it. Confucius, who lived in the far east about five hundred years before Christ, taught it. Philo, the philosopher theologian, imparted it. What is interesting, however, is that outside the Bible it is usually stated negatively.

Shami, a stern and rigid Jewish rabbi was approached one day by a pagan. "I am willing to convert to your religion if you can sum up your law while I am standing on one leg," the pagan said.

Shami drove the man from his presence with a big stick. I don't blame him. The man presented ridiculous conditions for becoming a convert.

The man then went to another rabbi, Hillel, with the same proposition. Hillel's response nailed the pagan. "What is hateful to yourself, do not do to others."

Tsze Kung, a disciple of Confucius, asked for one word that could be a rule for life. "Reciprocity," Confucius responded. "What you do not want done to yourself, do not do to others." That is often called the silver rule because it is negative. What we don't want others to do to us, we shouldn't do to them.

It is not a bad rule, but it isn't particularly religious. We don't have to embrace religion to recognize that it makes good sense. We don't have to endorse any ethical system, any theology, to understand that we can't live in society unless we follow that precept. It is little more than calculated shrewdness to avoid retaliation.

But Jesus was being positive. He said, "Therefore in everything, do to others what you would have them do to you, for this sums up the Law and the Prophets." In the Greek text and in many translations, the word *therefore* precedes the statement. The principle does not stand alone. It is not a nugget that we can take out of the Sermon on the Mount. The word *therefore* takes us back to what lies before.

At the end of Matthew 5, Jesus spoke about our relationship with others, which grows out of our relationship with God. And He summed it up by saying that we are to love our enemies, just as God does. God doesn't make the sun shine on only the good people. It shines on everybody. And we are to emulate that kind of goodness. When we love our enemies we are very much like God who does not discriminate.

In Matthew 7:11 Jesus concluded that the reason we go to God in prayer is because God gives us good gifts. So the word *therefore* refers to our relationship to God. Because God is our Father, because God is a good giver, because we are His children, we should be known for doing to others what we would have them do to us.

Although Jesus earlier commanded that we are to love our enemies, here He is even more specific. We are to do to others what we want them to do to us. In other words, we are to start with ourselves. We are to ask ourselves what we want the other person to do for us. I want the other person to be kind to me; therefore, I will be kind, I want the other person to be honest with me; therefore, I will be honest. I want people to help me when I am hurting; therefore, I will help them when they need it.

Conversely, I don't want people to make life difficult for me, so I will make it a point never to make life difficult for them. I don't want other people to bring out the worst in me, so I will endeavor not to bring out the worst in them. The important thing to note is that we are to take the initiative.

We are to govern our lives by doing for others what we want them to do for us. "This," Jesus said, "sums up the law and the prophets."

If you read the laws in the Old Testament with what Jesus said, you can see this connection to the Golden Rule. I recently went back to the Old Testament and read many of the laws. In doing this, I began to see the connection to the Golden Rule. For example, the law says, "Do not oppress an alien; you yourselves know how it feels to be aliens, because you were aliens in Egypt" (Exodus 23:9). There it is, the Golden Rule in the Old Testament. The Israelites should have known how to treat outsiders because they themselves had been outsiders. They were to treat strangers in the same manner they they themselves would have wanted to be treated.

Look at another example from the case law in Exodus. "If you come across your enemy's ox or donkey wandering off, be sure to take it back" (23:4). I don't own an ox, but if I did I wouldn't want it lost or killed. I would want the person who found it to be kind enough to bring it back to me. I, therefore, should do the same even if I find my enemy's ox.

What applied to oxen applied to donkeys. "If you see the donkey of someone who hates you fallen down under the load, do not leave it there; be sure you help him with it" (23:5). A donkey that has fallen under its load and unable to get to its feet is in grave danger. If that were my donkey, I'd appreciate it if somebody would help him get up so the poor beast wouldn't lie there paralyzed. If that's what I want someone to do for my animal, that's what I should do— without asking whose donkey it is, without weighing how the owner has treated me in the past.

The principle starts with us as a very practical application of the rule of love. It is active, not passive; positive, not negative.

The story of the Good Samaritan could have taken place in downtown Denver, Chicago, or New York. A traveler was stripped, mugged, and left in a pool of blood beside the road to die. Two men saw him but went on about their business. One was a priest and the other was a Levite. They practiced the silver rule. They didn't do evil to this man, but they didn't help him either.

If I were the victim I would want someone to aid me. I wouldn't care whether assistance came from a Jew or a Samaritan, nor would I care at all about the color of his skin.

We are not to help others because they have helped us. That is not how God deals with us. God's help has nothing to do with our merit. God doesn't love us because of what we are; He loves us in spite of what we are. We never have dibs on God. God doesn't owe us; He owns us.

Is the Golden Rule an absolute?

Probably not. We must be sure that what we want to receive from others is what we ought to receive. For example, I may want to be flattered, to have others say nice things about me whether or not they are true. So I flatter people to get them to flatter me. Eventually the whole process becomes destructive manipulation, and obviously that wasn't what Jesus was trying to generate.

Or suppose a man commits a very serious crime and is captured and brought to court. If I asked him what he would like the jury to do for him, no doubt he would say he wanted to be let off. That also would be true I'm sure of the jury members if they were guilty of a crime. Does the Golden Rule mean, then, that the jury should let the man go free? Should we always give people what they desire?

It is important to realize again that this is connected to the rest of the Sermon on the Mount, and the topic of the sermon is righteousness. Jesus was pointing out that we are to act righteously toward others so they will act righteously toward us. If we understand God's righteousness, we will not twist the Golden Rule into an excuse for unrighteous behavior.

If we walk with God, we are concerned about sin. The whole essence of the Sermon on the Mount is that when we recognize our desperate need, we come before God in mourning and we hunger and thirst for His righteousness.

If we fail to put the Golden Rule in the context of the Law and the Prophets and the Sermon on the Mount, we do great damage, instead of great good, to the society in which we live.

One other thing to remember is that the Golden Rule, as Jesus gave it, is a guide and not a goal. He was not saying we are to be nice to others so they will be nice to us. Receiving kindness from others should not be our motive for being kind. Although the Golden Rule expresses the way we are to conduct ourselves, it does not guarantee any results. In fact, early in the Sermon on the Mount Jesus alerted us against that expectation. "Blessed are you when people insult you, persecute you and falsely say all kinds of evil against you because of me" (5:11).

Several times in the Sermon on the Mount Jesus warned that people may take advantage of us, slander us, and persecute us if we live truly righteous lives. Let's be realistic: treating people kindly is no guarantee that others will treat us kindly. Chances are some people will take advantage of us. Living a godly life can put you at a disadvantage in the game of life. This doesn't mean, however, that we will necessarily come in last. We'll escape a great deal of disappointment if we realize that the motive for being nice isn't to get others to be nice to us. The golden rule is not a goal, it's a guide.

Then why do it? Because we live for the approval of our heavenly Father. It doesn't matter whether my enemy throws appreciation banquets for me after I bring his ox back to him. It doesn't matter whether others deal honestly with me after I deal honestly with them. We do not take our lead from the crowd but from our relationship with the Father. We represent Him to a society whose leaden rule is to do others before they do you. But if we are serious about our relationship with God, we live in love toward friend and foe, neighbor and enemy.

So I ask myself what I would want in any given situation. And when I answer that I don't ask further questions about the other person, I simply respond as God responds to me.

This is enough to make us uneasy. The Golden Rule should guide us in all our activities: at home in our relationships with our spouses and children; on the highway; at the football stadium; and in the office. It is not a precept we practice when it is convenient or when we want warm feelings.

When we sense our bankruptcy, our utter selfishness, we realize how seldom we put another person's interest first. When that hits us, we find ourselves driven back to the Beatitudes, the foundation of this sermon.

"Blessed are the poor in spirit, for theirs is the kingdom of heaven." I suddenly recognize how much I need the grace of God. "Blessed are those who mourn." When I strip away all my excuses, I realize that I am far from what God wants me to be; and I come with a sense of submission before God. A sense of deep need. And then I read, "Blessed are those who hunger and thirst for righteousness, for they will be filled." And out of that, 'Blessed are the merciful . . . Blessed are the pure in heart . . . Blessed are the peacemakers . . ." And I realize how being sure of my relationship with God affects my relationships with others.

Jesus was not telling me to turn over a new leaf. He was saying that this kind of righteousness demands a new life. He was not saying that I need to make up my mind to keep this rule. I can't do it on my own.

I recognize my desperate need for God's righteousness. I go to the Bible, but I can't keep all of God's rules and regulations. In fact, I can't even remember them all. How in the world can I reflect God's love? How am I to think? How am I to behave?

I am to determine that what I want others to do for me, I will do for them. I'll start by asking myself what I would want in that situation. Then I'll do it. The person who does that fulfills the kind of righteousness that God requires. And to do it consistently the person needs the righteousness that only God can give, righteousness that is a relationship of grace first with Him, and then with others.

Charlie Brown is a kind-hearted, do-good kind of character. Despite the abuse he receives from the other inhabitants in Charles Schultz's cartoon strip, *Peanuts*, Charlie Brown continues to practice the Golden Rule. Even though it rarely works to his advantage, Charlie Brown keeps doing for others what he would have them do for him.

In one strip Charlie and Lucy are lined up behind a bunch of other kids to see a movie.

"Have you been here long, Charlie Brown?" Lucy asks.

"No, I just got here. Actually, I shouldn't be going to the movies at all. I have homework to do. If it weren't for the fact that they're giving away free candy bars to the first fifteen hundred kids, I wouldn't even be here."

Lucy, who has been listening to the ticket agent counting kids while Charlie Brown talked, asks him, "Do you mind if I get ahead of you, Charlie Brown?"

"No, please do. 'Ladies first' is always my motto. I don't think this is a very good movie. I just came because of the free candy bars for the first fifteen hundred kids. I really should be home doing my reading, but you know how it is when they're giving something away free," Charlie Brown continues as Lucy pays for her ticket.

"Fifteen hundred!" announces the ticket agent. "Sorry kid, that's the way it goes."

The world is full of Lucys. When you practice the Golden Rule, don't do it for them; do it for your Father in heaven. He pays off with more than candy bars.

ELEVEN

SERVICE ENTRANCE

John Calvin profoundly influenced Christian faith. As a young man he was thoughtful, reverent, and studious. By age 27 he had written the first edition of his *Institutes of the Christian Religion.* By the time he died in 1564 he had laid down the planks for Reformed theology. In addition, he had laid some of the planks for democratic government. He died almost penniless, but measured by the standards of history he was a success. The treasure he gave the human race still enriches us today. John Calvin had a brother named Charles. Charles Calvin was a profligate. He led a desolate life. All that John Calvin was, Charles Calvin was not. He died a miserable wretch.

MATTHEW 7:13–14

What made the two men different? Not genetics. They came from the same parents. Not the environment. They grew up in the same home. Not education. They went to the same schools. In fact, in their early years they had nearly the same influences. But one man reached for the heights and the other didn't make it out of death valley.

What distinguishes us from one another are the choices we make. We make decisions and then those decisions turn around and make us. A lot of folks spend a great deal of money going to psychiatrists or therapists to find out who they are. But if we unpeel ourselves one layer at a time to find out who we are, we may end up with nothing more than what we get when we peel away all the layers of an onion: tears.

A playwright in New York City wrote an article about some of the men who had worked with him over several decades. He lamented the fact that many of them began with great promise but ended a lie. Summing up his observations he said, "In the final analysis very few lives are hits that end up on Broadway. Most lives are flops that finish out of town in New Haven."

His verdict holds a great deal of truth. Most people desperately want to be successful, but when life is over, measured by their own standards, they have failed. Why does that happen so frequently? We often blame heredity, environment, or genetics. Although all of those factors possess a shaping and molding force, they don't explain everything.

We are what we are committed to. If you tell me what you are committed to, I can tell you what you are. Certainly that is a theme of the Bible. Again and again biblical leaders call people to choose. Moses preached five sermons just before he died. Then he said, "This day I call heaven and earth as witnesses against you that I have set before you life and death, blessing and curses. Now choose life, so that you and your children may live and that you may love the LORD your God, listen to his voice, and hold fast to him" (Deuteronomy 30:19–20).

In Moses' audience that day stood a soldier named Joshua. When Moses died, Joshua took up the reins of leadership and led the people into the land God had promised them. When Joshua gave his farewell address he said, "Choose for yourselves this day whom you will serve, whether the gods your forefathers served beyond the River, or the gods of the Amorites, in whose land you are living. But as for me and my household, we will serve the LORD" (Joshua 24:15).

Moses and Joshua called the people of Israel to choose, and that has been true of preachers through the centuries. The really outstanding ones preached for a verdict. Someone said that a great sermon is a speech that ends with a motion to act. Effective sermons are not given for an audience to consider; they are preached to get people to decide. Jesus' preaching makes us nervous because He was asking for a radical decision.

Some people are attracted to Christianity because they have a leaky faucet and they want God to fix it. Perhaps they struggle with a destructive habit and they would like to tap God's power to help them break it. Or maybe they have broken relationships that they want God to mend. But they learn from the Sermon on the Mount that God is not a plumber. They learn that leaky faucets are minor league to Him. God wants to tear out the plumbing and deal with the well itself. He wants to change what comes out of the faucet. But really we want to settle for a minor repair, not a major renovation.

A friend of mine bothered by blurred eyesight went to her ophthalmologist to get a change of prescription in her glasses. He discovered a cancer behind her eye, a melanoma, and wouldn't even let her go home. He placed her in the hospital, removed the cancer, and treated her eye with radium. My friend wanted new glasses and ended up having radical surgery.

That is what Jesus does. His kind of righteousness isn't a prescription for glasses; He performs major surgery. We don't get His kind of righteousness with new glasses. We need major surgery. Jesus doesn't deal with leaky faucets; He deals with wells.

As Jesus delivered His sermon He wasn't preaching for applause. He demanded a decision. He pictured two gates, two ways, two trees, and two foundations. Travelers must choose their way; hearers their message; and builders their foundation. Listeners to Christ's message need to choose.

In Matthew 7:13–14 Jesus painted a scene depicting a narrow and a wide gate and a narrow and a wide way. The imagery behind those verses was common to someone living in the first century or to someone living today in the Near East. Most cities in the ancient world had walls, some wide enough for chariot traffic. And the walls of the city had gates. Jerusalem had twelve gates wide enough for two-way traffic. Throngs of people moved in and out to do their business and shop. In the ancient world those gates were closed at night. If the city came under attack, the doors would be shut against the invader. In the door itself or next to the gate there usually stood a small door to allow citizens known to the guards to enter at night. This helped the soldiers let citizens in while keeping enemies out.

Jesus had that image in mind. There are two roads and two gates, not three. We have a choice to make. If we have been listening to Him, we know that we are to enter the narrow gate and travel the narrow road. In fact, He told us that up front, just after the capstone was laid in the Golden Rule. "Enter," He said, suddenly, starkly, directly. It is a command. We are to enter the narrow gate and travel the narrow road.

That unsettles me a bit. I don't like to think of myself as narrow. Narrow people come through as dwarfed spirits with tunnel vision. Folks with no breadth to their lives. Country bumpkins who measure the whole world by their small towns. They have trouble seeing beyond their back fences. I think of narrow religious people in the same way. They measure everyone by their limited experience. They tell everyone what is wrong with the world, but they are not better, just smaller. Yet they think everyone is evil except them. They have a warped view of life and of God.

No. I don't want the reputation of being narrow. But in a sense truth is narrow.

When I was growing up I was not particularly adept at arithmetic. We usually studied it first thing in the morning, and I hated school because I dreaded that first hour. By the time I was six or seven, you see, I had developed an appreciation for broad-mindedness, but my arithmetic teacher didn't. She and her narrow math tables said that three times three equalled nine, but I took a more expanded view of arithmetic than that. I was willing to settle for seven, eight, or ten. Why be a stickler about one number more or less? That's why I never got into accounting. At the end of the day, week, or quarter if I were fifty dollars short, I would simply throw in the fifty bucks and forget about it. Good accountants don't do that. They tend to be narrow about numbers.

Narrowness not only governs math and accounting, but also it is an essential of marriage. When a couple stands at a marriage altar, they make a commitment. As their minister, I want them to enter into all the poetry of that relationship. I want to see it grow and develop. So I say, "Henry, will you take Agnes to be your lawful wedded wife, will you comfort her, cherish her, cling to her, forsaking all others, will you take her alone?" And Henry responds, "I will." That's limiting. Of all the women on earth he chooses Agnes. He makes a narrow commitment to her.

Some folks in our society don't like that restriction. They are broad-minded. That is one of the reasons homes get shattered and people wounded by the shrapnel—they have never grasped the narrowness of a deep relationship.

The way is narrow; the gate is narrow; the truth is narrow; our relationship with God is narrow. And narrowness, even in Jesus' day, was unpopular. In fact, so many people are surging down the highway to destruction that Jesus said only a few would find the narrow path to life. In other words, we can't find the right road by sampling majority opinion. The crowd does not applaud the individual who enters the narrow gate.

This can be disconcerting. All of us gain confidence when we surround ourselves with people who think the way we do.

Likewise, we lose confidence when we stand alone with our beliefs. Although some like smaller crowds than others, we all like the comfort of being with like-minded individuals. It's the "birds of a feather flock together" syndrome.

I don't like being the only Christian at an academic meeting and hearing speakers take cheap shots at the Christian faith. In fact, I don't appreciate it when I witness to the businessman next to me on an airplane who says, "You've got to be kidding me. You don't believe that, do you?" I don't like that at all. I like to play with the winners. I like to cheer for the champion. I'm not comfortable sitting alone. I don't enjoy being mocked for my narrow-mindedness when I tell people there is only one way to God—through Jesus Christ.

Our society is ripping apart at the seams because we poll the majority to define morality. If we expect to find truth by surveying the crowd, we will end up in disillusionment because the crowd consistently travels in the wrong direction. Going with the crowd is not the way to determine what really matters.

In the days of Athanasius, one of our church fathers, the great religious debate concerned the deity of Christ—whether or not Jesus Christ was God. It almost split the church. Orthodox Christians now believe that Athanasius was true to the Scriptures, but during his day he stood almost alone. People said to him, "Athanasius, give it up. The world is against you." To which Athanasius replied, "Then it must be Athanasius against the world."

When we make important decisions we must make them without considering whether or not they will make us popular. If popularity is our major concern, we are carbon copies of the Pharisees who lived for the applause of men instead of the approval of God.

Jesus warned us that the kind of life He is calling us to

invites persecution. People will say evil things against us, dismiss us as odd, or accuse us of parading our righteousness. Folks don't seek out friends whose life-styles show theirs to be wrong. If they live in darkness, they don't like what the light reveals. And rather than clean up their mess, they'll try to put out the light.

If we don't like to be narrow or unpopular, why choose the narrow road? We decide on the narrow road for the same reason we choose any road—for its destination. As Alexander McCartney said, "the main thing about a road is where it goes." Jesus said that the broad road leads to destruction. It may be an eight-lane, well-traveled highway; it may have beautiful scenery and marvelous accommodations along the way; it may be free of potholes. But Jesus said it ends in destruction. If we let the crowd decide our direction, we'll be destroyed with them.

The destination, not the road conditions, determines whether or not we're headed the right way.

Several years ago my son Torrey and I decided to go to the top of Mount Princeton, a 14,000-foot peak. Coming from New York City, I had never driven a jeep nor ridden on a mountain trail. I was not accustomed to hairpin turns that made me feel as if we were going headlong over the edge. Every time we turned another one I wished we had taken Highway 70 instead of the twisting trail. But Highway 70 didn't go to the top of Mount Princeton. To reach the mountaintop I had no choice but to take the jeep trail with its ruts and hairpin turns.

Likewise, Jesus said that only one road leads to life, and it's not a wide, well-traveled freeway. But we choose it—not for its comfort and convenience but for its destination. And when we do, we learn that folks who walk that narrow road are not narrow people. In fact, they are anything but narrow.

They are broad in their sympathies. They take the initiative to do things for others that they would want others to do for them. They do good to those who despitefully use them, and they pray for those who persecute them. They're concerned not only about family and friend, but also about foe.

They are broad in their purposes. They have sworn allegiance to another king and to another kingdom. They pray regularly, "hallowed be your name, your kingdom come, your will be done on earth as it is in heaven." Their purposes are not limited to their own concerns. They don't put their lives into their own houses, lands, or bank accounts. They live with a sense of the eternal. They take what is perishable and turn it into treasures that outlast them. They are not narrow in their goals.

They are also broad in their hopes. One of my major frustrations is that I want to do so many things and I know I don't have time to do them all. At times I look in the mirror and say to myself, "What's a young man like you doing in an old body like that?" Life for all of us ends more often with a whimper than a bang.

But if we are traveling the narrow road, our destination is life. Death is not the end of the road; it is a bend. Death is not a period; it is a comma. For us, the best is yet to come. We will do and be more than we ever dreamed possible.

No, the folks who choose the narrow gate and travel the narrow road are not narrow people. To walk with Jesus Christ gives us sympathies as broad as all mankind, purposes as great as heaven itself, and hope that is eternal.

To get on this road, however, we must make a choice. We don't stumble on to it by accident. We don't wake up one morning and discover that we are Christ's disciples. We become Christian men and women only when we recognize that we are bankrupt before God, that we possess a desperate hunger and thirst for righteousness. We recognize that we can't work up righteousness ourselves, and we cast ourselves with reckless abandon on the grace of God. We understand that God will make us merciful, will make us peacemakers, and will make us pure-hearted, which will mark us out in society as His children.

Our Puritan forefathers would not be overly impressed with some of our evangelistic methods: signing a card, raising a hand, or walking to the front of a church. They emphasized a covenant with God. In fact, they urged people to write out the covenant they had made with God as they would write out a business contract. They swore allegiance to a new king, to a new citizenship. They renounced their rights to themselves and gave themselves to God, to His work, and to His kingdom. Like enlisted soldiers, they gave up their rights to themselves and to their time. After writing the covenant they would sign it, seal it, and that would settle it. Not a bad thing to do.

When Charles Colson opened *Mere Christianity*, he found himself "face-to-face with an intellect so disciplined, so lucid, so relentlessly logical that I could only be grateful I had never faced him in a court of law," he wrote in *Born Again*. "Soon I had covered two pages of yellow paper with *pros* to my query, 'Is there a God?'"

The more Colson read of Lewis's mighty little book the closer he came to God. "I knew the time had come for me," he wrote. "I could not sidestep the central question Lewis (or God) had placed squarely before me. Was I to accept without reservations Jesus Christ as Lord of my life? It was like a gate before me. There was no way to walk around it. I would step through, or I would remain outside."

TWELVE

OUT OF TRUE

Years ago the Metropolitan Museum of Art in Amsterdam put some of their priceless originals next to copies and held a contest to see how many visitors could tell the false from the true. Of the 1827 people who took part in the experiment only seven were able to tell the genuine from the fake. What is true of paintings is true of prophets. People in our society believe their senses. So if something looks like a duck, waddles like a duck, and quacks like a duck, we believe it is indeed a duck. Generally that is true, but not always. If an animal looks like a sheep, sounds like a sheep, and is covered with wool, it is prob-

ably a sheep; but not necessarily. It may be a clever wolf.

Like a wolf in sheep's clothing, true and false prophets share many features in common. A lot of things we normally associate with true prophets can lead us astray.

For example, we cannot identify true prophets by the way they dress. They may or may not wear a clerical collar, a cassock, a cross around their necks, a business suit, or carry a Bible. They may have been ordained by some Christian denomination. They may flash all the credentials that go with ministry. Although they may exhibit the marks of a genuine calling, they may be false prophets.

Nor can we identify true prophets by their works, no matter how miraculous. Jesus said, "Many will say to me on that day, 'Lord, Lord, did we not prophesy in your name, and in your name drive out demons and perform many miracles?' Then I will tell them plainly, 'I never knew you. Away from me you evildoers!' " (7:21–23).

Evidently false prophets as well as true ones cast out demons, display spiritual powers, and perform miracles.

Judas, along with the other disciples, had power over the forces of hell. And speaking of the last times, Jesus said, "At that time if anyone says to you, 'Look, here is the Christ!' or, 'There he is!' do not believe it. For false Christs and false prophets will appear and perform great signs and miracles to deceive even the elect—if that were possible" (Matthew 24:23–24). Just because someone heals the sick does not mean he or she is a true prophet. We cannot identify true prophets by the miracles they perform.

Religious vocabulary is not a reliable test of true prophets either. The false prophets Jesus mentioned did all their works in His name. In fact, "in your name" is repeated twice in verse 22. Saying "Lord, Lord" was an important part of their religious vocabulary. But they were impostors. Jesus will say to them, "I never knew you."

True prophets perform their ministry in the name of Jesus, but false prophets also know how to use those words. We cannot tell them apart by their theological vocabulary. Just because a preacher on television speaks the name of Jesus does not necessarily mean he is a prophet of God. He may be a prophet of another power, using the right words to get across the wrong message. Historically, one way heretics brought false doctrine into the church was by using orthodox words but filling them with different meaning. Sometimes it is done deliberately, but not always. Some false prophets honestly believe they are right. We cannot distinguish authentic prophets from counterfeits by their vocabulary.

Perhaps even more disturbing is that we cannot identify true prophets by their sincerity. False prophets are not necessarily charlatans who intentionally use a religious message to line their own pockets. Quite often they are dedicated. They build churches, raise money, preach decent sermons, and do it all in a sincere way. In fact, they are so sincere and effective that when they stand before God they will be shocked to discover that the God whom they thought they represented does not know them at all.

It is difficult to distinguish the false prophets from the true. It is hard to spot the counterfeits from the original. We cannot tell them by the clothes they wear, the ministry they perform, the words they speak, or even their sincerity.

So how do we identify the prophets of God? How do we separate them from false prophets? Jesus answered that question twice. "By their fruit you will recognize them," He said in verse 16 and again in verse 20.

We usually apply this passage to morality. We assume Jesus was saying that we can identify good people by their good deeds, by the lives they live. But having studied so much of the Sermon on the Mount, we know that cannot be what Jesus was teaching. In fact, some of those He singled out as being false prophets, the Pharisees and the scribes, kept all the religious rules and regulations. If "fruit" means the same as "good works," the Pharisees would be the first to qualify for a medal of righteousness.

Many cultured people in the world do good deeds and don't even pretend to be Christians. And many men and women who live moral lives make no time in their schedules for religion. No, we can't know the authenticity of prophets merely by examining the quality of their conduct.

The fruit of an orange tree is an orange. The fruit of an apple tree is an apple. The fruit of a grape vine is a grape. And the fruit of a prophet is prophecy. The primary question about a prophet is whether or not his teaching is true to the Word of God. Is the word of the prophet the same as what Jesus preached in His Sermon?

Throughout the Old Testament, the litmus test of a prophet did not lie in his ability to predict the future. And it had nothing to do with scolding the congregation. Today when someone says "He has a prophetic message" they usually mean that he speaks with a pious snarl and severely criticizes the world and the church.

The test of a prophet was always whether or not he spoke for God accurately.

A true prophet teaches what Jesus taught. He tells us that we stand before God bankrupt, that we have nothing to give God to a acquire right standing with Him. He does not tell us to straighten up and get our act together or to turn over a new leaf. He does not urge us to simply shape up our moral conduct. The true prophet preaches that we have something radically wrong deep inside us. That's why Jesus started His Sermon by saying "Blessed are the poor in spirit, for theirs is the kingdom of heaven." A true prophet makes us aware of the depth of sin in our lives. And this awareness makes us feel a sense of mourning about our sin. "Blessed are those who mourn, for they will be comforted." This mourning leads to a craving for righteousness. "Blessed are those who hunger and thirst for righteousness, for they will be filled."

The true prophet does not tell us to conform to a list of rules and regulations. He doesn't tell us how to dress or how to wear our hair. True prophets deal with what we are inwardly. They make us aware of who we are before God. So when we give, fast, pray, or worship, we don't do it to impress the minister, the deacons, or our spouses. We don't do it to be an example. We do it because our Father who sees in secret will reward us. True prophets make us concerned about His approval.

His righteousness not only gives us a relationship with

Him, it gives us a relationship with others, a relationship of love, a relationship out of a pure heart. We become aware that anger and homicide are not that far apart. The seed of unresolved anger can yield the weed of murder. Lust can flame into immoral conduct, divorce, ruined families, and shattered relationships.

God's righteousness at work in our lives produces genuine concern about integrity. Our promises don't depend on contracts written by shrewd lawyers. We deal honestly because we want to please God. And our honesty makes us merciful, pure in heart, and peacemakers.

The message of the Bible doesn't have to do with self-image, self-help, success, making money, winning, or staying healthy. Its truth has to do with our sinfulness before God and being made right before Him, and that comes about because Jesus Christ who preached this sermon went out and died to make it happen. He paid the penalty for all our sin.

Ultimately there are only two kinds of religion in the world: the kind that we have to carry and the kind that carries us. Religion that we have to carry—that depends on our strength, determination, and zeal—belongs to the false prophets. The religion of the Bible carries us. It depends on what Christ has done to declare us righteous.

Beware of false prophets Jesus cautioned. They are here today; they were there nineteen hundred years ago. We can hear them on the radio or watch them on television or see them in front of a church. We cannot recognize them by their vocabulary, their effective ministry, or their sincerity; we can only measure them by their prophecy, by their fruit.

The first question Jesus asks of me is, "Are you staying true to my Word?" The second question He asks of me is, "Is your life true to the Word you preach? In the day of judgment people will expect many of their actions to pass muster with God, but they won't make it at all. People who have been involved in religious work, who have learned all the right phrases, have carried on religious missions, and have preached moving sermons will hear from Jesus Christ, "I never knew you. Away from me, you evildoers!"

A soul is a dangerous thing to lose. We had better be careful whom we listen to, whom we watch, and what we read. Some who seem like gentle sheep may be ravenous wolves.

Elmer Gantry was a fictional example of a great deceiver. When Sinclair Lewis wrote his novel in 1927, many Christians felt he had sensationalized the story of the corrupt evangelist. Unfortunately, it has turned out that Lewis was a prophet of sorts. Elmer Gantry could substitute for one of a number of modern-day preachers.

Gantry, though guilty of immorality, deception, and hypocrisy, eventually discredited his accusers and, in the last scene of the book, faced his congregation.

"Without planning it, Elmer knelt on the platform, holding his hands out to them, sobbing, and with him they all knelt and sobbed and prayed, while outside the locked glass door of the church, seeing the mob kneel within, hundreds knelt on the steps of the church, on the sidewalk, all down the block.

"'Oh, my friends!' cried Elmer, 'do you believe in my innocence, in the fiendishness of my accusers? Reassure me with a hallelujah!'

"The church thundered with the triumphant hallelujah . . ."

And so do thousands of deceived believers today. But Jesus Himself is not in the crowd.

THIRTEEN
FOUNDATION

Twenty-five years ago I had a conversation with a Dallas homebuilder, a Christian who tried to make his faith effective in his business. My friend believed it was important to build good houses with solid foundations, sturdy walls, and good insulation. He paid attention to details the buyer couldn't see. Other builders, however, were more con-cerned with get-ting business than with building qual-ity homes, so my friend was losing to the competi-tion. His competi-tors knew that the couples buying homes were pri-marily concerned with appearance —bric-a-brac and decorations. This placed an honest

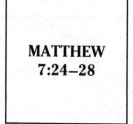

MATTHEW
7:24–28

builder at a disadvantage. If he gave attention to the founda-tion and put insulation in the walls and attic, he didn't have money for many decorative touches. If he put in the decora-tions, he had to raise his prices. What bothered him most was that the folks buying the homes didn't care about what was hidden. They only expected to live in the houses a cou-ple of years, so appearances meant more to them than quality.

My friend solved his problem by getting out of the residen-tial building business and getting into commercial property. Buyers there were more interested in what was put into the foundation, the walls, and the roof.

A few years ago I was back in Dallas and I drove through the neighborhood where my friend had tried to build homes. It looked like a slum. When we don't pay attention to what is hidden, a time comes when what is hidden will be revealed.

At the conclusion of the Sermon on the Mount, Jesus expressed concern about good housing. That should not sur-prise us; He was a carpenter. As part of the firm of Joseph

SOLID

and Sons in Nazareth, He had built the furniture that people put into their houses and He had probably built some of the homes as well. Jesus knew the difference between a solid building and a shoddy one. Therefore at the end of the Sermon on the Mount, this carpenter-preacher talked about sensible and stupid builders.

In the last illustration in His sermon, Jesus described two men who had built homes. The builders had several things in common. First, both were building permanent houses. They weren't putting up toolsheds or erecting tents. They wanted to settle down, raise their families, and pass on a home to their children.

They were probably building similar dwellings as well. Jesus put no emphasis at all on any difference in design. For all we know they may have used the same blueprints—same plates for the windows, chimney, porch, doors. They may have been situated in a slightly different position on the ground, but for Jesus' purposes the two buildings could have been identical. The differences would not be seen by the average person. The houses looked the same. The casual observer could not see there were different foundations. Although that difference was not obvious, it was fundamental.

One man built his house on a foundation of rock, the other put his house on a foundation of sand. It seems like a scene from the theatre of the absurd. It is difficult to imagine anyone stupid enough to build a house on sand. But the picture is not as absurd as it appears. In early summer many of the areas in Palestine, or even in the United States, look like lovely places to build homes. The land is smooth, the view is magnificent, and the sandy plain baked by the sun looks like an inviting place to live.

Besides, building on sand takes a lot less. Digging into the rock requires more sweat and time. Erecting mansions on the sand has distinct advantages and that's why people build there today. On the West Coast people build their homes on or next to faults. Others build on the cliffs overlooking the Pacific Ocean. They have a marvelous view of the sunset. But when a storm comes it eats away the ground underneath the house, and some of those lavish homes slide down the hill. Some actually tumble into the Pacific. Even after such disasters others insist on constructing houses on the slippery hillsides again.

Storms, Jesus said, reveal the difference between houses that appear identical. The pounding rain reveals the stability of the foundation; the wind tests the strength of what we have built.

When we review the Sermon on the Mount, we recall that Jesus wasn't very concerned about appearances. They can be deceiving. In His preceding story Jesus talked about guarding against wolves in sheep's clothing. False prophets and authentic ones also resemble one another. They speak the same language, wear the same clothes, carry on the same kind of ministry. The foundational difference is their prophecy.

When Stanford University was built, it had a great arch like the great Roman victory arches. It was built in memory of Leland Stanford, who gave an enormous amount of money to start the university. That arch, built so grandly, solidly, and splendidly, looked as if it would stand forever. But when the earthquake came the arch collapsed in ruins. Apparently the builder had tried to save some money. Instead of building that arch of solid rock and going as deep as he could go, he erected it on top of rubble. The earthquake revealed the builder's wretched choice.

Obviously, Jesus wasn't talking about the construction business. Nor was He giving instructions on how to build houses. He was driving home a lesson on building a life. Although we can use many pictures to describe our lives, Jesus chose a building metaphor. Our lives resemble houses. Everyone is building a house of some sort. But our lives are not just made up of brick and wood, nails and mortar. All of us have a foundation for our lives. Something on which we build. It may not be much more than shifting sand or it may be solid as a rock.

Some people build their lives on possessions—how much they own. Some build their lives on passions—the satisfaction of desires. Some build their lives on position—the jobs and offices they hold. And some build their lives on what is eternal.

All of us are building a life according to some scheme, some design. We don't build at random. We all have a world view. We all have a philosophy. We all have something important to us on which the building blocks of our lives rest.

Jesus said all of us will have the foundation of our lives tested. All of us—wise builders and foolish builders, Christians and atheists—will be exposed to the storm. Christians don't get a free pass. God doesn't pamper His people. The benefit of being a Christian is not protection from the hurricanes that blow our way in life.

The storms are what test us. Living in the sunshine of life doesn't tell us much about ourselves. Anybody can build a house that will stand firm when the sun is shining and the wind is still. It is the storms that reveal the strength of our foundations.

Sometimes the storm breaks us with the fury of a great temptation. In the last two weeks I've had conversations with men undergoing enormous temptation. One man, who works for a financial institution, has debts he cannot pay. He has access to the funds at work and is tempted to "borrow" some. He intends, of course, to pay them back before anyone finds out. Another man is strongly tempted to throw aside his marriage, his family, and his reputation. He is romantically overwhelmed by a young woman he knows. What we really are is exposed by the storm of temptation.

Sometimes the storm is a crushing personal loss. You may lose a job that not only provides income but also provides you with self-esteem and personal security. A carefully built stock portfolio suddenly destroyed can be like a tornado roaring through the comfortable life you have built for yourselves. When we realize that we haven't built up the security we counted on and everything in our life comes tumbling down, we see exposed the faulty foundation of our lives.

Sometimes the storm roars in as we are pounded by sickness or the fear of death. You can lose your health and anguish, pain, and the prospect of death may come between you and the leisurely retirement you've anticipated. You begin to question the strength of the life you've built. And when someone you love goes out into the mystery of death, a not-so-solid foundation can start coming apart. Times like these reveal the foundations of our lives.

For others, the foundation is tested by prosperity. Prosperity comes to us like a gentle spring rain. At first we're convinced it will make our lives green and healthy. But when prosperity keeps coming, it can develop into a large destructive force as damaging as a storm. What we gain, not what we lose, often serves as the supreme test of our foundation. More men and women have been knocked off their spiritual foundation by great wealth than by great reversal.

For all of us there comes the storm of judgment as certain as the fact of life, of death, of God Himself. We will all stand at the judgment bar of Christ and give an account for the living of our days. That storm will be the final test of whether our foundation is rock or sand, whether we have built on what is secure or on what is fleeting.

We are all building, Jesus declared, and what we are building will be tested, not in the sunshine but in the storm.

The third thing Jesus conveyed is that some will stand while others will fall. Jesus said that those who hear His words and practice them build wisely.

Many religious people deceive themselves into believing that knowing the Bible is the same as obeying it, that memorizing verses is the same as applying them, that assenting to the doctrines of Christ is the same as practicing them. Jesus said "not so." To hear the Word is essential, of course, but to *do* it is to know it. We must know our desperate need of God, and then we must cast ourselves upon Him to supply that need. We must know we are dependent on God, but then we must be obedient as well. The center, the focus, the foundation of our lives must be Jesus Christ. People who build on that foundation will stand when the storm comes. In the day of judgment that foundation will hold us secure.

But not all houses will stand. In fact, the Sermon on the Mount ends with a severe note of judgment. We like sermons that end positively, on an upbeat note, that send us away feeling good about ourselves. But Jesus issued a storm warning at the end of His sermon.

Jesus had a lot to say about judgment and hell. In His sermon He mentioned two doors, two roads, and two voices. Those who choose the broad way will end up in destruction, and those who follow the false prophets will be like refuse thrown into the fire. In chapter 5 Jesus talked about hell and compared it to Gehenna, the garbage dump outside Jerusalem. He pictured judgment and its destruction like being thrown on the garbage dump of the universe.

Jesus used all kinds of images—darkness, fire, a garbage dump—to tell us that destruction is coming for those whose houses don't stand. God takes us very seriously, even though we may not take ourselves seriously. But the decisions we make and the foundation on which we build has eternal implications. We are not flotsam and jetsam. We are not leaves tossed about by the winds of life. We make choices, and they make us what we are. And those who choose to build on sand will one day find their house has crumbled.

Therefore, we must not only be careful how we build, we must choose carefully what we build on. What is the foundation of our life? What really matters to us? That's what will be revealed at the judgment.

When we take a friend to church with us, one of the first questions we ask after the service is "What did you think?" We want to know if our friend liked the sermon, the preacher, and the service. Most of us don't hear the rave review that Jesus got. In Matthew 7:28 we learn that his hearers were astonished by His teaching. They were amazed at two things: the matter and the manner of His teaching.

They were astounded by what He taught. He differed from anyone they had heard before. He didn't urge them to new forms of religion, to give more money, or to attend services more often. He didn't summon them to a greater commitment to a religious routine. He kept going back to their motives, to what they were deep inside. He said that what mattered to God was their relationship with Him. He said that true religion wasn't a performance, it was a deep reality. Out of it came complete trust in God, and out of that came a love that would cause them to seek the highest good for others.

That wasn't the religion of the first century and frankly it isn't the religion of today. Our religion emphasizes ceremonies and attendance, things that don't matter much, and it ignores the weightier matters of what we are deep inside.

In addition to their astonishment at the matter of His teaching, the people were impressed by the manner in which He taught: He taught as one having authority, not as the teachers of the law. Rabbis were highly educated. They knew their two thousand years of religious tradition inside and out, and they had studied all the learned opinions. But they did not teach as if they had authority. In most of their teaching they simply quoted the experts. Listening to them was like listening to someone read an extended footnote.

Jesus didn't teach like that. Standing two thousand years away from the Sermon on the Mount, we may not appreciate the significance of this difference. Jesus was about thirty years of age, not very old by the standards of the ancient world. He had grown up in Nazareth, a small town of little importance. When Nathanael heard that Jesus came from Nazareth, he said, "Can anything good come from there?" (John 1:46). Jesus was a carpenter, an artisan. He had not gone to the schools the rabbis had attended. He had never studied the religious traditions. And yet, at thirty years of age, this son of a carpenter, from a fifth-rate little village, spoke with an authority that the older scribes and the teachers of the law did not possess.

When the prophets spoke in the Old Testament, they introduced their message by saying, "Thus saith the Lord." That little phrase appears almost three thousand times in the Old Testament. The prophets did not speak with their own authority; they spoke with the authority of God. It is striking that Jesus never used that phrase. He spoke with His own authority.

In Matthew 5:17 Jesus said that He had come to fulfill the law. In His own life, by the way He lived, He embodied all that the law pointed to. Not only in actions, but in motives. In addition Jesus said that He fulfilled all of the Old Testament, all of its prophecies pointed forward to Him, all of its promises related to Him, all of its history ultimately touched on Him, and all of its future depended on Him. He was the one of whom all the prophets spoke. And He Himself would be the judge of all people.

The judge of all the earth preached this sermon. And eternal destinies will be decided by what people do with Him and what He does with them. He spoke with authority all through the Sermon when He interpreted or reapplied the law, when He promised, when He commanded, when He prohibited. Not in the name of God, but as God himself. The people had never heard anyone do that because no one like Him had ever appeared on earth before.

After studying the Sermon on the Mount, we recognize it is not merely another moral code. It has a way of condemning us, of revealing our motives, of unscrewing the top of our hearts and looking in. And we come away, as Jesus said in the first beatitude, with poverty in spirit, which drives us back to Him.

When the Sermon ended the people were driven back to Jesus. They were astonished by the content and the manner of His teaching. In the end, any sermon worth preaching drives us back to Jesus Christ. Christianity doesn't exist without Him. The essence of Christianity is a relationship to a person, not to a code of conduct. A relationship to a Lord, not to a law. And that's an eternal foundation; He's the only base on which we can safely build our lives.

After a disagreement with World Vision board members, Bob Pierce, founder of the relief organization, signed away his life's work.

"I gave them everything—my films, my office, my work. I

told them if they wanted it so badly they could have it. I started with nothing; I'll leave with nothing," Pierce explained to his family after his decision.

In *Days of Glory, Seasons of Night*, Pierce's daughter, Marilee Pierce Dunker, described the family's reaction.

"Jesus was still the foundation our lives were built upon, the solid Rock which is the same yesterday, today, and forever," Dunker wrote. Yet she also said, "Suddenly there were no clear-cut definitions, because the thing that had controlled and defined the purpose of our existence—the ministry—was gone . . .

"Everything had emanated from that—our friends, our family relationships, our attitude about ourselves. We lived in that quiet assurance that we belonged to something truly remarkable, something that . . . gave our lives a special meaning and purpose."

Jesus said that when we build our lives on anything other than Himself—even a religious cause—we risk losing everything. Dunker described her father during those days as "a king exiled from an empire of his own making. He mourned his loss with angry bellows and stormy silences, and we all watched with growing concern as his inward turmoil began to manifest itself in uncontrollable shaking and choking spells."

Pierce's ten-year-old daughter, Robin, spoke for the whole family the day she asked, "Who are we now, Mama?"

Those who belong to the solid rock construction company always know whose they are.

Note to the Reader

The publisher and author invite you to share your response to the message of this book by writing Discovery House Publishers, P.O. Box 3566, Grand Rapids, MI 49501 U.S.A. For information about other Discovery House publications, write to us at the same address.